# STARTING WITH HEIDEGGER

Continuum's *Starting with . . .* series offers clear, concise and accessible introductions to the key thinkers in philosophy. The books explore and illuminate the roots of each philosopher's work and ideas, leading readers to a thorough understanding of the key influences and philosophical foundations from which his or her thought developed. Ideal for first-year students starting out in philosophy, the series will serve as the ideal companion to study of this fascinating subject.

**Available now:**

*Starting with Berkeley*, Nick Jones

*Starting with Derrida*, Sean Gaston

*Starting with Descartes*, C. G. Prado

*Starting with Hegel*, Craig B. Matarrese

*Starting with Hobbes*, George MacDonald Ross

*Starting with Nietzsche*, Ullrich Haase

*Starting with Rousseau*, James Delaney

*Starting with Sartre*, Gail Linsenbard

**Forthcoming:**

*Starting with Hume*, Charlotte R. Brown and William Edward Morris

*Starting with Kant*, Andrew Ward

*Starting with Kierkegaard*, Patrick Sheil

*Starting with Leibniz*, Lloyd Strickland

*Starting with Locke*, Greg Forster

*Starting with Merleau-Ponty*, Katherine Morris

*Starting with Mill*, John R. Fitzpatrick

*Starting with Schopenhauer*, Sandra Shapshay

*Starting with Wittgenstein*, Chon Tejedor

# STARTING WITH HEIDEGGER

TOM GREAVES

continuum

For L & R

Continuum International Publishing Group
The Tower Building                80 Maiden Lane
11 York Road                      Suite 704
London SE1 7NX                    New York, NY 10038

*www.continuumbooks.com*

British Library Cataloguing in Publication Data
A catalogue record for this book is available from the British Library.

ISBN: HB: 978-1-8470-6139-3
PB:  978-1-8470-6140-9

Library of Congress Cataloging-in-Publication Data
A catalog record for this book is available from the Library of Congress.

Typeset by RefineCatch Limited, Bungay, Suffolk
Printed and bound in Great Britain by
the MPG Books Group

# CONTENTS

CONTENTS

CHAPTER 10   ART AND SCIENCE: POETRY
AND THOUGHT                                            139

# ABBREVIATIONS AND REFERENCED WORKS

References give the pagination of the English translations listed below, followed by the corresponding German pagination. Translations have occasionally been modified. Occasionally, references are made to numbered sections of the texts marked §. In *Being and Time* these sections and headings were devised by Heidegger, in lectures and manuscripts they are usually provided by the editor of the German *Gesamtausgabe* (Complete Edition) volumes. Works from this edition are marked below as GA, followed by the volume number.

## WORKS BY HEIDEGGER

BCAP    *Basic Concepts of Aristotelian Philosophy*, translated by Robert D. Metcalf and Mark B. Tanzer (Bloomington: Indiana University Press, 2009)/GA 18: *Grundbegriffe der aristotelischen Philosophie* (Frankfurt a. M.: Vittorio Klostermann, 2002).

BPP     *The Basic Problems of Phenomenology*, translated by Albert Hofstadter (Bloomington: Indiana University Press, 1988)/GA 24: *Die Grundprobleme der Phänomenologie* ((Frankfurt a. M.: Vittorio Klostermann, 1997).

BT      *Being and Time*, translated by John Macquarrie and Edward Robinson (Oxford: Basil Blackwell, 1962)/ *Sein und Zeit* (Tübingen: Niemeyer, 1993).

BQP     *Basic Questions of Philosophy: Selected 'Problems' of 'Logic'*, translated by Richard Rojcewicz and André Schuwer (Bloomington: Indiana University

|  |  |
|---|---|
|  | Press, 1994)/GA 45: Grundfragen der Philosophie: Ausgewählte 'Probleme' der 'Logik' (Frankfurt a. M.: Vittorio Klostermann, 1984). |
| CP | *Contributions to Philosophy (From Enowning)*, translated by Parvis Emad and Kenneth Maly (Bloomington: Indiana University Press, 1999)/GA 65: *Beiträge zur Philosophie* (*Vom Ereignis*) (Frankfurt a. M.: Vittorio Klostermann, 1989). |
| EGT | *Early Greek Thinking*, translated by David Farrell Krell and Frank A. Capuzzi (New York: Harper & Row, 1975). |
| FCM | *The Fundamental Concepts of Metaphysics: World, Finitude, Solitude*, translated by William McNeill and Nicholas Walker (Bloomington: Indiana Universty Press, 1995)/GA 29/30: *Die Grundbegriffe der Metaphysik. Welt-Endlichkeit-Einsamkeit* (Frankfurt a. M.: Vittorio Klostermann, 1992). |
| HCT | *History of the Concept of Time: Prolegomena*, translated by Theodore Kisiel (Bloomington: Indiana University Press, 1992)/*Prolegomena zur Geschichte des Zeitbegriffs* (Frankfurt a. M.: Vittorio Klostermann, 1979). |
| IPR | *Introduction to Phenomenological Research*, translated by Daniel O. Dahlstrom (Bloomington: Indiana University Press, 2005)/GA 17: *Einführung in die phänomenologische Forschung* (Frankfurt a. M.: Vittorio Klostermann, 1994). |
| KPM | *Kant and the Problem of Metaphysics*, translated by Richard Taft (Bloomington Indiana University Press, 1997)/GA 3: *Kant und das Problem der Metaphysik* (Frankfurt a. M.: Vittorio Klostermann, 1991). |
| MFL | *The Metaphysical Foundations of Logic*, translated by Michael Heim (Bloomington: Indiana University Press 1992)/GA 26: *Metaphysische Anfangsgründe der Logik im Ausgang von Leibniz* (Frankfurt a. M.: Vittorio Klostermann, 1978). |
| N1 | *Nietzsche, Vol 1*, translated by David Farrell Krell (London: Routledge & Kegan Paul, 1981) & Vol 2. translated by David Farrell Krell (New York: Harper |

         & Row, 1984)/GA 6.1: *Nietzsche I* (Frankfurt a. M.: Vittorio Klostermann, 1996).

OBT     *Off the Beaten Track*, translated by Julian Young and Kenneth Haynes (Cambridge: Cambridge University Press, 2002)/*Holzwege*, 4th edn. (Frankfurt a. M.: Vittorio Klostermann, 1963).

OHF     *Ontology – The Hermeneutics of Facticity*, translated by John van Buren (Bloomington: Indiana University Press, 1999)/GA 63: *Ontologie (Hermeneutik der Faktizität)* (Frankfurt a. M.: Vittorio Klostermann, 1988).

OWL     *On the Way to Language*, translated by Peter D. Hertz and Joan Stambaugh (New York: Harper & Row, 1971)/*Unterwegs zur Sprache* (Pfullingen: Neske, 1971).

PIA     *Phenomenological Interpretations of Aristotle: Initiation into Phenomenological Research*, translated by Richard Rojcewicz (Bloomington: Indiana University Press, 2001)/GA 61: *Phänomenologische Interpretationen zu Aristoteles: Einführung in die phänomenologische Forschung* (Frankfurt a. M.: Vittorio Klostermann, 1985).

PLT     *Poetry, Language, Thought*, translated by Albert Hofstadter (New York: Harper & Row, 1971).

PM     *Pathmarks*, edited by William McNeill (Cambridge: Cambridge University Press, 1998)/*Wegmarken* (Frankfurt a. M.: Vittorio Klostermann, 1996).

PRL     *The Phenomenology of Religious Life*, translated by Matthias Fritsch and Jennifer Anna Gosetti-Ferencei (Bloomington: Indiana University Press, 2004)/GA 60: *Phänomenologie des religiösen Lebens* (Frankfurt a. M.: Vittorio Klostermann, 1995).

PS     *Plato's Sophist*, translated by Richard Rojcewicz and André Schuwer (Bloomington: Indiana University Press, 1997)/GA 19: *Platon: Sophistes* (Frankfurt a. M.: Vittorio Klostermann, 1992).

QCT     *The Question Concerning Technology and Other Essays*, translated by William Lovitt (New York: Harper & Row, 1977).

SAGU      'The Self-Assertion of the German University', in *Philosophical and Political Writings*, ed. Manfred Stassen (New York: Continuum, 2003).

Supplements    *Supplements: From the Earliest Essays to 'Being and Time' and Beyond*, edited by John van Buren (Albany: State University of New York Press, 2002).

TDP      *Towards the Definition of Philosophy*, translated by Ted Sadler (London: Continuum, 2000)/GA 56/57: *Zur Bestimmung der Philosophie* (Frankfurt a. M.: Vittorio Klostermann, 1987).

VA      *Vorträge und Aufsätze* (Stuttgart: Neske, 2000).


### OTHER FREQUENTLY CITED WORK

CPR      Immanual Kant, *Critique of Pure Reason*, translated by Paul Guyer and Allen W. Wood (Cambridge: Cambridge University Press, 1998).
[Citations refer to the standard pagination given in the margins of this edition]

# PREFACE

The aim of this volume is to give the reader an idea of the scope of Heidegger's work, while at the same time focusing attention on the matter that he was trying to think through and the range of ways that he tried to do so. Heidegger taught his students again and again that philosophy is not ultimately about learning doctrines or positions, but about provoking and allowing oneself to be provoked into thinking. To that end this introduction does not run through the themes and concepts of Heidegger's first major work *Being and Time* in precisely the order that they are there dealt with there, nor does it strictly follow the chronological order of Heidegger's philosophical development. The chapters very roughly follow the order of presentation in *Being and Time*, but the material is frequently rearranged and I do not cover every point in that text. I also draw upon the large and increasing number of texts that are now available in German and English, especially lecture courses and manuscripts from before and after the composition of *Being and Time*, to show how Heidegger approached the matter that needs thinking through from various angles and in various ways. I have also occasionally sought to draw out Heidegger's thoughts in ways that are not strictly his own, but which should afford the reader some space for doing likewise when coming to an understanding of what he wrote.

As will become clear, Heidegger understood philosophy as unavoidably engaged with its own history. There is perhaps no other philosopher who engaged in such depth with such a wide range of other thinkers, not only philosophers, but mystics, poets, artists and scientists. To write a full history of the influences on Heidegger's thought would be to write a history of a great deal of European, and not a negligible amount of Eastern, intellectual history. I hope to have given some indication as to how Heidegger took up and transformed the thoughts of a number of thinkers of particular significance to him. Many more remain in the background. One of these is the philosopher and poet Friedrich von Hardenberg, known as Novalis, from whom the epigraphs to each of my chapters originate. They can be found in *Novalis: Philosophical Writings*, translated by Margaret Mahony Stoljar (Albany, N.Y.: State University of New York Press, 1997). Heidegger read Novalis a number of times throughout his career and clearly found in his work an echo of and provocation for his own thought.

I would like first of all to thank David Wood for suggesting that I write this book. Thank you to Sarah Campbell and Tom Crick at Continuum for their support and great patience. Heartfelt thanks also to all the teachers who have stimulated and guided my engagements with Heidegger, especially to Miguel de Beistegui, who opened up many new horizons. There are many friends with whom I have read and struggled with Heidegger over a number of years. Thank you to them all. Friends, and teachers from Sussex, Warwick, Freiburg and beyond, have all helped to enable my understanding. More recently, colleagues at the University of East Anglia have been enormously supportive. In particular, thanks to Oskari Kuusela, who has been a genuine mentor. Many thanks to all those who looked out for me along the way and allowed me to start this book on its way to arrival. I take full responsibility for the outcome.

# INTRODUCTION

**start** *v.* Probably before 1200 *sterten* move or spring suddenly, in Layamon's *Chronicle of Britain*; later *starten* (before 1325); perhaps developed from Old English *steortian* or *stiertan*, variants of *styrtan* to leap up (about 1000); related to *starian* to STARE. Old English *styrtan* is cognate of Old Frisian *sterta* to overturn or overthrow, Middle Low German *storten* to overthrow or fall, Middle Dutch and Dutch *storten* to spill and throw, Old High German *sturzen* to fall or throw (modern German *stürzen*), Middle High German *sterzen* stand stiffly or move briskly, and Old Icelandic *sterta* to stiffen or strengthen, from Indo-European *(s)terd-/(s)tord-/(s)t̥rd* – (Pok.1023)

The sense of awakening suddenly is first recorded about 1386, and that of flinch and recoil in alarm, before 1325. The meaning of cause to begin acting or operating is first recorded in 1666, in Pepy's *Diary*, and specific sense of begin to move, leave, depart in Scott's *Kenilworth* (1821).

*Chambers Dictionary of Etymology*

Martin Heidegger thought a great deal about what it means to start out in philosophy. Anyone who begins to read his work will soon be struck by a peculiar feature of his way of philosophizing; the great significance that he attributes to the history of words. Throughout his philosophical career he frequently started out on a train of thought by pointing to some long forgotten meaning of a word. One reason for this is that he was always trying to remind us of the simple fact that thinking takes place not just in language, but in a specific language, with all of its own idiosyncrasies and historical twists and turns. Philosophers have often tended to suggest that this is a rather unfortunate state of affairs, a state of affairs which we may not be able to overcome, but which must be striven against, in so far as we want to achieve clarity about our own use of words and the matters under investigation. Heidegger, on the other hand, understood the historical and idiosyncratic character of language as our primary resource for thinking. We must always start from where we are and we are always in the midst of things and words, already 'in the thick of it,' as we say. There is no clear and obvious, universally valid, point of departure or destination for philosophical thought. Philosophy can help us to get more fully into the thick of things and words and find ways through that we had never discovered before.

Many of the historical meanings for the verb 'start' given above are echoed at various points throughout Heidegger's writings. From the Danish philosopher Søren Kierkegaard he took up the theme of a 'leap' of understanding and existence that serves as its own ground and justification. Heidegger also claimed that a true start in thinking must concern itself with overturning philosophy as it has traditionally been practised. This does not mean that we can simply put the history of philosophy to one side and start anew. Our whole way of thinking is so permeated by this history that any attempt to do so would simply result in our taking up the same problems and employing the same concepts, with less clarity about where we are coming from and what we are attempting. Overturning of philosophical thought must come from within the history of that thought (Chapter 9). Heidegger also thought that we are always starting in the sense of 'falling', since it is a basic tendency of our existence to lose itself in a familiar world and in general opinions about how to get on in that world (Chapters 3 and 4). We flinch and recoil from fundamental attunements, such as anxiety and profound boredom, that can shock us out of that familiar absorption. Yet philosophy seeks to jolt us awake by bringing us to fully experience such attunements (Chapter 5).

In all of these ways Heidegger was a philosopher who was always starting and who urged us to start out on our own, offering us many indications and suggestions as to how we might do so. Yet, one might well want to ask right away whether this is really a satisfactory way to view the various senses which are packed into the word 'start', or any other word for that matter. In this way we might find all sorts of strange, wonderful and completely irrelevant senses of key philosophical terms that will lead us completely off track. Is philosophy then to become the unpacking of various arcane word meanings that are completely unrelated to one another, that just happen to have ended up being called by the same name, and then spinning out some strange and completely unjustifiable tales about them?

After all, if we apply this method to the word 'etymology' itself, we discover that it is rooted in the Greek words *eteos* and *logos*, 'true' and 'word' or 'sense'. Are we to gather from this that etymology gives us the true sense of a word? Who would be so naïve as to suggest that the first meaning must also be the final word? Or that a word signifies today what its ancestor signified 2500 years ago? Or that we should regulate word use so as to stick as closely as possible to the 'original' meaning? How are we even to know when we have actually reached the original and primary meaning? With further investigation, we may always find a connection leading us further back. All in all, this would appear to be an absolutely hopeless method for teaching us anything about what our words mean today, let alone helping us to come to any relevant and penetrating philosophical insight.

So why does Heidegger appeal to ancient word meanings so often and why have I started off this introduction to Heidegger's thought by recalling some of the history of the word 'start'? Rather than taking us back to the only proper and true meaning of a word, a rock solid ground from which to begin philosophical reflection, these appeals are, on the contrary, attempts to loosen up hardened concepts and to show us that our words can and do mean more than we ever thought they could. To understand this a little better, we can consider an image devised by one of Heidegger's most important philosophical inspirations and interlocutors, Friedrich Nietzsche. Whilst complaining that we are far too quick to assume that there is a single unity and root concept in words such as 'revenge' and 'value', Nietzsche once exclaimed in exasperation: 'As if all words were not pockets into which now this and now that has been put, and now many things at once!'[1] Words signify many things, some of which result from our using them in particular ways, but there is also a huge and undiscovered trove of meaning in the language that we use both for everyday purposes and in philosophical thought. The appeal to the history of words is not an attempt to find their one true meaning, but on the contrary, to allow ourselves some access to the nuance and complexity of meaning in what is being said and has been said.

In a late essay Heidegger claimed that the Greek term *logos*, word or sense, can be traced back to speaking, *legein*, and that this in turn can be understood as laying out and gathering together.[2] Our words and concepts gather things together and show them as belonging together, but in such a way that they are not necessarily identified as mere examples of a general form or particulars subordinated to a universal. If our words have conceptual unity, then that is not because all of their meanings derive from a core meaning and a set of hard and fast rules for understanding, but because disparate meanings have been gathered together. *Logos* is the performance of this gathering. If we want to learn how to lay out and gather concepts in this way, then we need to learn first of all how they have been brought together in the past and to recognize difference and disparity in their unity.

There is, however, a certain danger in this way of going about things, which Heidegger was not unaware of. When, as we will see in Chapter 6, he points us towards the Greek word for truth, *alētheia*, and translates it as uncovering, Heidegger claims that this gives us a better sense of the depths of truth than theories that concentrate on the truth value of propositions. There is a risk here, but Heidegger thought that philosophy would be failing in its task of finding and preserving a language to express what is most crucial to us as human beings (beings that Heidegger calls 'Dasein'; open, questioning beings, for which see Chapter 2) if it refused to run this risk:

> In citing such evidence we must avoid uninhibited word-mysticism. Nevertheless, the ultimate business of philosophy is to preserve *the force of the most elemental words* in which Dasein expresses itself, and to keep the common understanding from levelling them off to that unintelligibility which functions in turn as the source of pseudo-problems.[3]

Many readers of Heidegger have come to the conclusion that it is precisely 'uninhibited word-mysticism' that he failed to avoid. Even Maurice Merleau-Ponty, a philosopher who had the greatest respect for Heidegger and learnt a great deal from his way of going about philosophizing, felt that he sometimes fell into this trap: 'Too quickly trusting language, he would be the victim of an illusion of an unconditional wisdom contained in language, and that we would possess only by practising it. Hence the false etymologies of Heidegger, his gnosis.'[4] As readers of Heidegger, if we are prepared to learn from him, but are not simply prepared to take his word for it, we need to decide whether he was able to remain true to the ultimate business of philosophy as he understood it or whether he fell prey to the force of his own words. Making that decision will be the task we set ourselves in engaging with Heidegger's thinking, while if we ever come to a point where the decision has been made once and for all, then it seems likely that we will have little more to learn from Heidegger's way of thinking.

# CHAPTER 1

# PHENOMENOLOGY: THE LOGIC OF APPEARING

All that is visible clings to the invisible. That which can be heard to that which cannot – that which can be felt to that which cannot. Perhaps the thinkable to the unthinkable.

*On Goethe*, 30

Phenomenology is concerned with how things appear. This makes it importantly distinct from other philosophical enterprises, which tend to assume that how things appear is obvious and that we need to ask more searching questions in order to really get a grip on things. For example, in Plato's dialogues, Socrates often asks his interlocutors what a particular phenomenon is, whether it be justice, or virtue, or knowledge. He is not content with a description of the sorts of things that are just or virtuous or with examples of knowledge, but rather he is looking for a definition of what it is that makes each of these things just, virtuous or known. Philosophy thus conceived begins with a search for the determination of *what* things are. Aristotle frequently began with a somewhat different line of questioning, asking *why* things are as they are and *why* certain processes occur as they do. He thus began to orientate philosophy towards a search for the causes of things. However, in doing so he also began to think about what a cause is and developed a well-known theory distinguishing four different kinds of cause. So he was still concerned, in looking for causes, with the determination of *what* the phenomenon of causation is. Phenomenology on the other hand, according to Heidegger, is less concerned with the determination of what things are than with the characterization of *how* they are. With this concern phenomenology develops philosophy on a very different footing to that set out by the Greeks, although

6

that Greek thought was in effect often phenomenological, showing us *how* phenomena make their appearance, even if it did not comprehend itself as such.[1]

One problem that phenomenology faces in trying to characterize *how* things make their appearance is precisely that it can seem all too obvious. We expect things to appear in a certain way, expectations which are built up from habit and traditional theories about how things are. These expectations are so powerful that things really do appear in conformity with them. To take a simple example, as I think of a walk I took this afternoon through a meadow I know well, it appears to me at first that the grass was a lush green color. It may even have appeared that way at the time. This is because, as everyone knows and as I have seen in this very meadow many times before, grass is green. However, if I had looked carefully at what was before my eyes today and if I recall it carefully now, I see the purple-red color of the seed heads that make their appearance in high summer. I see the meadow as it appears and not as I think it should appear or must appear. Phenomenology sets itself the task of trying to resist much more deeply engrained prejudices about how the world and the things in it really are and to get us to look more carefully at how they appear. Yet it is not a purely descriptive exercise, if that means an attempt to give a basic characterization of how things appear at first sight, before we go on to develop a theory to explain them. A preliminary characterization of how things seem will inevitably be informed by and directed by prejudices and expectations. An adequate characterization of how things appear requires that we do not remain content to let things appear in the light of those expectations. As Heidegger's mentor Edmund Husserl put it: 'What is needed is not the insistence that one see with his own eyes; rather it is that he not explain away under the pressure of prejudice what he has seen.'[2]

## i. PHENOMENOLOGY WITHOUT ATTITUDE

It was Husserl who, towards the turn of the twentieth century, began to develop this idea of phenomenology as a philosophical project. He began his career as a mathematician and when he moved into philosophy became interested in logic. Rather than being primarily concerned with the formal structure of arguments he was interested in how and why the things that were investigated by 'pure logic' actually turn out to be structures of the world as we experience it. This became a problem for him after he was convinced that logic is not simply the psychological result of the way human minds happen to be set up and the habits of thought that those minds have acquired. If logic remains 'pure' in the sense that it is not concerned with how particular minds happen to think about the world, then we are faced with the problem of showing why the world as we experience it does conform to the rules of logic. It was in answer to this problem that Husserl developed the idea of phenomenology in a two volume treatise *Logical Investigations*, published in 1900. Phenomenology was to be an investigation into how phenomena make their appearance and into how the logical rules of thought contribute to the way things appear and are actually found in a proper description not just of how we happen to think, but in the basic structures of our engagement with phenomena. Heidegger came across the *Logical Investigations* as a student, when he was himself interested in very similar issues of how and why it is that pure logical categories actually apply to the world as it is experienced. He was always drawn to thinkers who were convinced that the problems of logic should not be allowed to become problems of abstract self-contained theoretical systems, that can then be applied to specific problems in epistemology or metaphysics after the fact of experience. Of primary interest was the way logical categories arise from experience and how such categories originally contribute to making our experience what it is.[3]

Husserl always understood phenomenology as fulfilling a traditional ambition to make philosophy into a rigorous science. However, he came to think that this science was of a quite different kind to all of the other sciences, not only natural sciences but human sciences as well. How this difference should be understood became for him one of the central problems of phenomenological research. In a treatise entitled *Ideas Pertaining to a Pure Phenomenology and to Phenomenological Philosophy*, first published in 1913, Husserl addressed this problem by claiming that all other sciences develop a theoretical attitude out of what he called the 'natural attitude'.[4] While other sciences are concerned with a particular 'domain' of things, there is no special kind of entity or domain of things that phenomenology is concerned with. Rather, it is a question of a difference in attitude. It is not *what* is investigated, but *how* it is investigated which distinguishes positive and phenomenological science. What then is the phenomenological attitude? It involves a shift that allows us to suspend the implicit judgments that we have always made in advance about how things have to be and how they have to show up, so as to see them as they actually do show up. The most basic of all the assumptions of the natural attitude is its positing of a world of things in their actuality. In positive scientific investigation, we may discover that things are quite different to how we naïvely imagined them to be at first. Nevertheless, in this attitude things are always posited as being already and actually there, such that they may become available for investigation. Husserl claimed that the natural attitude that posits the actuality of things in this way, along with a set of prior assumptions about what kinds of things there can be, is generally assumed when we look at and encounter the world around us. Phenomenology attempts not simply to discard that attitude and its accompanying assumptions, but to work against them with an increasingly radical series of what Husserl calls 'reductions', that 'bracket' or 'suspend' them.[5] We thus shift ourselves into a radically different attitude that is free to see how the phenomena appear rather than allowing its entire concern to revolve around establishing what is real or unreal among the phenomena.

Heidegger was inspired and convinced that the phenomenological project was a crucial new attempt to delineate what philosophical research should be trying to achieve. Nevertheless, he was not content with the idea that what distinguishes the way that we engage with phenomenology from everyday and theoretical discourse should be understood as a shift in attitude. This idea itself, he argued, makes unwarranted assumptions about the conditions under which things usually appear to us. The idea of a shift in attitude implies that we begin with a certain kind of attitude towards the world which was not phenomenological, that is, the natural attitude. The condition for the appearance of phenomena, *how* things show up, is that we take up an attitude towards them. In everyday life, according to Husserl's analysis, we have already done this. The task of phenomenology is to shift our attitude, so that we can take a critical distance from our natural attitude. It is above all the idea of a natural attitude that Heidegger took issue with:

Is this natural attitude perhaps only the semblance of one? This kind of comportment and experience is of course rightly called an *attitude* [*Einstellung*], inasmuch as it must first be derived from natural comportment, from the natural way of experience; one must so to speak "place oneself into" [*hineinstellen*] this way of considering things [and so assume an attitude towards them] in order to be able to experience in this manner. Man's natural manner of experience, by contrast, cannot be called an attitude.[6]

It is essential for phenomenology to begin with the characterization of our everyday understanding of the world and the things we encounter in it, if it is to see its own attempt to transform that understanding in the right way. However, the idea that the appearance of things is always the result of an *attitude* implies a position taken up in the face of the phenomena under investigation, moreover, a position which the investigator has put herself in, even if not as a matter of mere choice. The German word *Einstellung*, here translated as attitude, reflects this as it contains the root *stellen*, positing or setting in place. It is the word which today is used to mean the *settings*, for example, on a computer program. Settings are the basic framework which we lay down, within which particular things appear and can be manipulated. It would not be too much of an exaggeration to say that Heidegger's philosophical struggle was always an attempt to free us from the positions, theses, sets of principles and dogmas that we lay down for ourselves both in encountering things in the world and thinking about those encounters. Years later he would identify *setting* as the essential feature of the technological age, which affects the way we understand thinking, production and nature itself, as we will see towards the end of this book in Chapter 10. If we want to understand how human beings naturally encounter the world and consequently how our way of seeing things changes when it becomes phenomenological, this will not be achieved in terms that understand us as already positioned over and against the world and the things in it. Furthermore, the attitude that Husserl thought we take up towards the world, even before theoretical and scientific investigation, seems to be geared towards the project of *knowing* about the things in that world. The subject encountering the world is understood as taking up a certain attitude and its primary concern is to develop the correct method for *knowing about* the phenomena that show up. According to Heidegger, on the other hand, it is the project of gaining theoretical knowledge that involves taking up a position *vis-à-vis* the world and cannot legitimately be read back into our natural or everyday existence. It is because Husserl always had scientific knowledge in view, even if he claimed that phenomenological science differed from positive science, that Heidegger argued he was led into a misunderstanding of natural 'pre-scientific' existence. It is possible to have a phenomenology of theoretical knowledge, because this is one way in which things appear to us. Still, we should not assume or allow ourselves to be guided by the prejudice that we can adequately characterize how we are primarily engaged with things in terms that involve our taking up a position towards them and thus positing them as objects of investigation.

Husserl was still in the grip of a certain theoretical prejudice that manifested itself in his characterization of what phenomenology as a philosophy must try to achieve: 'Husserl's primary question is simply not concerned with the character of the being of consciousness. Rather, he is guided by the following concern: *How can consciousness become the possible object of an absolute science?*'[7] While Husserl's phenomenology does not take the actuality of the things that show up in consciousness for granted, it does take the field of consciousness in which they appear for granted and thus makes assumptions about the presence and availability of this field as an object for scientific treatment. For Heidegger, an adequate characterization of how we are engaged with things when they appear to us must constantly work against all of the attitudes and standpoints that we tend to assume towards them.

## ii. THE ROOT OF SENSE AND SENSIBILITY

For both Husserl and Heidegger phenomenology is concerned with characterizing the basic ways in which we encounter things, an investigation that is at one and the same time an investigation into how those things become manifest to us. Husserl had designated this as an investigation into *intentionality*. Consciousness consists of acts that are always directed towards something, something that it 'intends'. Phenomenology is not primarily interested in what is intended, but in characterizing how this directing ourselves towards things brings about their appearance.

One of the most important sources for this account of the philosophical enterprise was Immanuel Kant's *Critique of Pure Reason*.

Kant had argued that philosophers should not concern themselves with trying to demonstrate what the real world is like above and beyond all appearances. Rather, they should be concerned with giving an account of how things come to appear to us. Although Kant makes an important distinction between 'appearances' and 'things-in-themselves', that distinction can be understood as one not between two different worlds, but between the same world considered in two different ways. If we simply think about the world independently of all apprehension of it, then we are thinking about it as it is in itself. If we apprehend the world in any way at all, so that things appear to us in some way, then we are thinking of that same world as it appears.[8] Appearance is not simply an illusion, but the world as it appears to us.[9] Illusions are a particular kind of appearance that do not fit together in a way that makes them intelligible. Kant tried to discover how it is that things that appear can be intelligible, and in this sense he was already engaged in phenomenology.

Kant's investigation of how things appear turned on a distinction that he makes between two human abilities: the first an essentially passive and receptive faculty of sensibility through which we receive what he calls 'intuitions'; the other an essentially active intellectual faculty through which we are able to understand and make intelligible what we receive from sensibility. Our intellectual faculty of understanding uses 'pure concepts' to understand what is received, concepts that are not derived from what we receive. These concepts Kant calls 'categories'. So, for example, we understand changes in things as having causes because we actively subsume things under the category of causation, which we did not derive from seeing changes occur. Unlike rationalist philosophers who claimed we can gain substantive knowledge by simply thinking about the nature of things, or empiricists who had claimed that we could experience things purely receptively, Kant claims that we have no experience of things at all unless both the passive ability to receive and the active ability to understand things are working together. A large part of Kant's project in the *Critique of Pure Reason* is, then, to work out precisely in what forms things are received, what the categories are by which we understand them and how these two abilities to receive and to understand are able to work together to produce experience.

Heidegger was particularly concerned with how the two Kantian faculties are brought together in experience. Husserl had already argued in *Logical Investigations* that there is such a thing as 'categorial intuition', which Heidegger understood to be one of the great discoveries of his phenomenology.[10] For Kant, the best clue to find out what the categories are and thus the contribution that they make to the appearance of things in experience was to be found in formal logic and its treatment of judgments. Husserl's idea is that the constitutive acts whereby we are able to understand what we apprehend are already operating in our direct perception of things, in our seeing, hearing, touching and so forth. In that case, while categories of the understanding are not simply received from the world, they are operating in our reception of it and so the best clue to discover what they are and how they contribute to appearance is to be found in that intuitive apprehension itself. We can, if we are able to see phenomenologically, literally see our thought at work in the way things appear. This opens up a vast field of investigation into 'pure consciousness' that looks into the contributions of the thinking and understanding subject to what is seen, by carefully describing how things appear. Kant's procedure, by contrast, restricted the acts that make things intelligible to a narrow set of pre-prescribed rules for making judgments about them. Nevertheless, the idea of categorial intuition does not clear up the problem of whether it is possible to think of receptive sensibility and active understanding as originating together in our way of encountering things, a problem that was to preoccupy Heidegger.

In his book *Kant and the Problem of Metaphysics*, published in 1929, Heidegger argues that this problem can be addressed by returning to Kant himself. We can, he argues, return to the root of the problem of how things appear to us by looking again at what Kant says about the two faculties that are the sources of that appearance. He finds that Kant actually suggests that these faculties, although quite distinct, might have a common root.[11] If we can understand that source then, instead of simply positing two faculties and trying to see how they work together, we might achieve a more basic characterization of how experience comes about. For Heidegger, Kant actually gives us a clue as to what this common root might be in his own account of how the two faculties are brought together in experience. The key is what Kant calls the 'transcendental power of imagination'. This should not be understood as what produces the 'merely imaginary' or unreal, but as what allows for the formation of all appearances, including the real and the imaginary.[12] According to Heidegger's interpretation, it is not simply a third faculty alongside the other two, but the root power from which the other two spring and which allows for their conjoining in experience.[13] The transcendental power of imagination that is in us opens up a field in which things can be encountered and thus is not itself a purely passive reception of things or an active intellectual grasping of them. It is the source of both of those faculties together. It is with the characterization of this root power that opens up and cultivates 'the range of possible appearing as such'[14] that Heidegger thought we must concern ourselves. Kant, however, having once recognized this power at the root of receptive sensibility and active sense-making understanding, later shrank back from it and assimilated it to the spontaneous activity of the intellect.[15]

At the root of receptive sensibility and spontaneous active understanding Heidegger finds the core power of experience, what we might call a radical *negotiation* that is neither wholly passive nor wholly active. Acts of intentionality turn out to be negotiations. What does that entail? Negotiation takes place in discussion, not simply as reception of what the other wants to say nor as a purely active positing of what is being said in my own terms, but as an active responsiveness to what is being said. Negotiation also has the sense of 'negotiating a terrain' that involves both the powers that I bring with me to make headway and the adaptation and perhaps significant alteration of those powers in the face of what I encounter on the way. All of those powers that we usually associate with 'consciousness', such as sense perception, judging and conceiving, are embedded within lives that are fundamentally characterized as the opening up and negotiation of a field of possible 'sense', where sense is prior to and at the root of receptive sensing and active making-sense of things.

### iii. CONCRETE SKETCHES OF EXPERIENCE

Given this reorientation of phenomenological research away from what appears and towards characterizing how the field of possible appearance is opened up and negotiated, how does Heidegger understand philosophical concepts? Is there any real difference between philosophical concepts and any other concept? Heidegger's answer is that philosophical concepts are not extracted from experience but neither are they functions or rules that can operate independently of experience. The idea that he began to develop early in his philosophical career was that philosophical concepts are *formal indications.*

In an early lecture course from 1919, published under the title *Towards the Definition of Philosophy*, Heidegger started to tackle a deep-seated concern that theoretical concepts seem unable to do, so as to do justice to our lived experience. If this is the case then that is a major objection to a phenomenology that wants to characterize such experience. For phenomenology must, of course, make use of words and concepts in its characterizations and if those concepts necessarily take us away from our concrete experience, then phenomenology would seem to be an impossible undertaking from the start. Heidegger agrees that theorization tends to 'de-vivify' our lived experience. It does this in quite a specific way: 'I call it *the specific level-boundedness of the steps in the process of devivification.*'[16] The de-vivification of experience in this manner of conceptualization is 'level-bounded' because it involves generalization that takes place in steps. So, for example, we move in generalizing steps from 'red' to 'color' to 'perceptual experience', from 'house' to 'dwelling' to 'building', or from 'horse' to 'animal' to 'living being'. That is not to say that those concepts at the bottom of this stepwise generalization are not themselves general; they are. 'Red', 'house' and 'horse' are themselves general concepts, and there is no way of proceeding backwards in the process of generalization to arrive at a concept that does not have general application. What is taking place here is the classification of generalities within wider generalities, of species within genus. In lectures from 1920, Heidegger characterizes generalization as a 'way of ordering' and 'encompassing': 'Generalization is thus ordering; it is determination from another, such that this other belongs, as *encompassing*, to the same material region [*Sachregion*] as that to be determined.'[17]

The fundamental problem arises when all conceptualization is taken to be generalization. Must every conceptualization be a generalization and thus removed from concrete lived experience? Remarkably, Heidegger's solution is to claim that phenomenological characterizations are not generalizations but *formalizations.* We may think that the general and the formal are similar and that the formal is in fact an extreme generalization through which we have proceeded to remove all specific content from the concepts we began with. However, formalization does not have the stepwise level-bounded character of generalization, but rather it is something that is achieved all at once. Formalization in formal logic and mathematics, for example, is not achieved by extreme generalization. A formal symbol like 'x' can be replaced by anything of any level of generalization. However, if formalizations are simply place-holders for general classifications then they are still bound to the ordering and encompassing of domains.[18] Phenomenological 'formal indications', on the other hand, are formal characterizations of experience that are not bound to generalization. For example, we have just seen that Heidegger characterized the experience of theoretical generalization as the 'ordering' and 'encompassing' of a domain of things. That is not itself a generalization; it does not say that generalization belongs to a class of acts that orders and encompasses. It opens up and indicates to us the character of generalization, allowing the concrete manifestations of that experience to become apparent.

Can we say anything about our lived experience without killing it? De-vivification is not the inevitable fate of all attempts to put our experience into words. Rather than entering into the step-by-step de-vivification, we can move *all at once* to the formal indication of that experience. These formal concepts are 'indicative' because they do not set us up in an attitudinal stance towards the things or try to order them within a pre-delineated domain that encompasses them. Rather, formal indications are a way of drawing our attention and allowing something to appear freely for us. For example, if I am out on a walk with a friend I may draw her attention towards a particularly spectacular view with an open gesture of my arm, or perhaps an exclamation: 'Look at that, fantastic!' With such a formal gesture or remark, I allow the scene to make its appearance freely and in a fully concrete and lived experience. On the other hand, if I remark, 'Look at that, what an interesting example of the kind of valley created in this region by glacier movements' or 'Look at those grape vines that are also to be found in such and such a country . . .', then I have begun the process of encompassing and ordering what is experienced in a complex matrix of generalizations.

We might think of a formal indication as something like an artist's sketch. Indeed in his 1929 book on Kant, Heidegger describes the way that a concept even as simple as a house can be the 'initial sketching-out [*Vorzeichung*] of the rule' yet, 'is no list [*Verzeichnis*] in the sense of a mere enumeration of "features" found in a house'.[19] In sketching one does not simply try to 'get down' what has already come to light in a complete experience, but concentrates one's attention on how things are coming to light. A sketch is not like the rough draft of a work that tries to completely capture an experience, but the opening up of a field for experiencing that is then worked through. In this sense even a 'complete' work, like a painting, remains a sketch so long as our engagement with it, as artist or spectator, is one of opening up and working through this field of experience. By contrast, our experience and the conceptualization inherent in experience often become more closely akin to painting-by-numbers. Such painting can also be a creative engagement with the phenomena, but it takes place within an established and pre-set framework in a way that the sketching out of experience does not. That framework itself ultimately had to be sketched out, but in painting-by-numbers it becomes the self-evident framework within which experience unfolds.

The thought that philosophical concepts are indications or sketches should not be taken to suggest that they must remain utterly vague gestures or bare outlines. A simple gesture or remark is an invitation to begin further detailed indication of the precise character of experience. By concentrating our attention a sketch concretizes experience. It is the *concentration* of experience in formal indication that makes philosophical concepts concrete. Indeed, Heidegger thought that this led philosophy to become *concrete* research, properly understood as compressing our experience of phenomena, rather than as filling out an abstract scheme with material content:

Concrete work indeed signifies: to approach the object in its concrete form. What does "concrete" mean here? To clarify the sense we must intentionally free ourselves from the determinations of "formal" logic, where "abstract," *abstractum*, is understood in the quite definite sense of general material logic and in relation to which the sense of *concretum* and "concrete" is established. Instead we will adhere to the word. The concrete or, more precisely, that which is said to exist "concretely" is that which is condensed and originates out of compression, compaction. Insofar as an object is possessed concretely, the possession is related to the object in such a way that it grasps the determinations of the object fully and in their full jointure and compaction, i.e., properly grasps the ultimate structural sense of the full object in the richness that determines what and how it is.[20]

Whereas form is usually understood in opposition to content, so that concrete thinking is understood as filling out an abstract theoretical form, no such opposition arises in the case of philosophical concepts understood as formal indications. To do 'concrete work' in philosophy is not to fill out abstract theory with specific examples. If there are examples in philosophy, then they form part of the indication which compacts and compresses the full richness of the phenomena. The phenomena can then be understood in their 'full jointure and compaction', the way that they appear not as abstractly related, but concretely joined in experience.

Formal indication is thus a way in which phenomena can be approached; the formality of the concepts is the very way in which they are indicative of concrete experience, making it a unified 'approach-character'.[21] The difference between formal indications and theoretical generalizations is ultimately not one of different kinds of thing. That would be to think of concepts precisely in terms of the ordering and encompassing of generalization. The difference is one of approach and what one is trying to achieve in conceptualization. One is an approach that tries to order and encompass experience and the other an approach that tries to sketch out a field in which experience can be concretized. However, any conceptualization can be taken as an attempt at ordering and encompassing of a domain of things in generalizations. Thus philosophical concepts are always open to radical misunderstanding and misinterpretation, not because they are necessarily more obscure or abstract than any other concepts, but because we do not recognize the way in which they demand that we approach the phenomena.[22] Phenomenology is above all about approaching things in the right way. The right way is the way that allows them to appear as they are, without impelling us to grasp them by ordering them and encompassing them in generalization. If we fail to pay due attention to this then we will constantly misunderstand how phenomenological indications work and what they are trying to achieve. Although Heidegger complains that Husserl went astray when he characterized phenomenology as setting oneself up in a specific attitude towards things, phenomenology is about cultivating the right 'attitude' if we bring to the fore the root of the English word in the Latin *aptus*, to fit. Phenomenology is about cultivating an apt approach to things so that experience can be concretized, rather than about settling on a fixed response, a correct method, which is then deployed in order to grasp what we already have in view.

## iv. THE SELF-EVIDENCE AND ELUSIVENESS OF PHENOMENA

We approach phenomena in philosophy with words, either spoken or written, and the search for a fitting approach is therefore at one and the same time a search for fitting words and concepts. In fact, we are always approaching phenomena with words and concepts even if we are unaware of doing so, or of the need to find those that are fitting. That clearly does not mean that we always have to be talking about things in order for anything to show up at all. Nor does it mean that we are always aiming towards such an explicit articulation. It does mean that the possibility of providing such an articulation is always there because we already understand what appears in a certain way. Every approach we make to the phenomena and every manifestation of the phenomena can only take place in and through what the Greeks called *logos*, a logic of appearance that does not come after the fact but allows us to experience things in the first place. In the introduction to *Being and Time*, his major treatise published in 1927, Heidegger offers us a preliminary conception of phenomenology in which he looks at the Greek roots from which that name is composed – *phainomenon* and *logos* – and finds an 'inner relationship' between them.[23] A *phainomenon* is that which 'shows itself in itself', and *logos* is a 'letting-something-be-seen'. So it turns out that the characterization of *how* things make their appearance and of *how* they can be fittingly approached form an indissoluble whole in phenomenological investigation.

The consequence of this inextricable relationship between the self-showing of phenomena and the *logos* that allows them to appear is that there could never be a completely lucid and perspicuous view of things any more than there can be words that explain and elucidate everything. While phenomena show themselves in themselves, in doing so they cover over something else. In elucidating something in one way, we inevitably cast it into shadow in another. Ultimately it is not other things or aspects of themselves that appearances cover over when they appear, but the whole field of possible appearance within which those things show themselves. Things appear in that field, and in doing so draw attention away from the field itself. In an early sketch of the relationship between self-showing of phenomena and *logos*, Heidegger designates the fact that neither appearances nor the discourse that allows them to appear are self-evident as the *elusiveness* of the being of the world.[24]

Phenomenology remains for Heidegger an investigation into the 'logic' of appearance. But now, rather than being a solution to the problem of why things apparently conform to logical rules and principles once they have come onto the scene, phenomenology tries to understand the *logos* that allows things to become apparent in the first place. The same prejudice tends to inform our approach to the phenomena and the *logos* inherent in them, that the way things come to appearance is self-evident and self-explanatory. We do not fall into that prejudice through foolishness or chance. When things have already appeared on the scene we forget the scene in which they make their appearance and they do appear as self-evident. When we have already understood something we forget the discourse within which it became intelligible and it becomes self-explanatory. Everything appears to be already open to view and if something is obscure then that obscurity might in principle be fully removed, allowing the self-evident presence of things to shine through. If we are once able to remove ourselves from this prejudice then we will see that appearances are never fully present, that our understanding is never complete and that what is needed is an ever renewed effort to allow things to appear and to understand them as they are through interrogation of what is apparently self-evident.

# CHAPTER 2

# DASEIN: A LIVING QUESTION

The transcendental point of view of this life is awaiting us – there we shall find life really interesting for the first time.

*Miscellaneous Observations*, 49

Heidegger wanted to address what he saw as the neglected question of the being of intentionality, which is simultaneously the question of the being of phenomena. To reveal the being of phenomena at all requires interrogation and questioning. Where should this questioning begin? Heidegger's claim, obvious as it might seem, is that we must always start from where we are. That is self-evident, but what is not self-evident is precisely what kind of being we ourselves have, such that there is a 'where I am' and 'where we are' in and through which phenomena become apparent to us. What kind of being has a 'there' of this kind from which it must always start? What kind of being can ask about where it is and what it means to be open to what is 'here'?

## i. INTERROGATING OURSELVES

In the introduction to *Being and Time* Heidegger argues that we must start our interrogation of the being of phenomena by interrogating ourselves. We are the starting point, because we are the ones who are able to ask the question:

Looking at something, understanding and conceiving it, choosing it, access to it – all these ways of behaving are constitutive ways of behaving for questioning, and so are themselves modes of being of those particular beings which we, the questioners, are each of us ourselves. Thus to work out the question of being adequately, we must make a being – the questioner – transparent in its being. The very asking of this question is an entity's mode of *being*. This being, that we each are ourselves and which has questioning as one possibility of its being amongst others, we shall denote by the term *"Dasein"*.[1]

Why does Heidegger propose this terminology for the being that we each are ourselves? It is a term that is usually left untranslated from the German and means in everyday usage the 'being' or 'existence' of anything at all. Heidegger reserves it to denote only our own way of being. Most importantly for Heidegger the term is composed of two parts and in later texts he often highlights this with hyphenation, *Da-sein*. *Sein* is 'being', while *Da* can mean 'here' or 'there'. When asked where something is to be found, one can point to it and say 'Da', meaning 'it is here' or 'it is over there'. However, for Heidegger it is not some particular location, but the whole open field in which things can appear that is the 'Da' that belongs to our being. It is the 'where I am' and 'where we are' that belongs to each of us.

Heidegger's claim here is that questioning gives us a clue as to the kind of being that is open to this field that is 'there'. The first thing to notice is that questioning can take many forms and involves many specific activities. Questioning is not simply formulating a sentence with a question mark at the end of it, but involves looking carefully into something, selecting it as the thing to be asked about and coming to understand any potential answer to our question. The ability to formulate sentences that have question marks at the end and others that are answers is one kind of ability that can form a part of questioning. Questioning does not begin and end with the formulation of questions. Instead, it begins with the recognition of something that we want to understand and continues, in the seeking of an answer. It also continues in the formulation and reformulation of questions and answers, as we reveal certain things about what is being interrogated and also recognize that certain other things are being obscured.

Although questioning is one possibility among others for this being that we each are ourselves, it is not an ability which it just happens to have. The ability to question turns out to be a clue to the way that Dasein exists, to what kind of being it has. Questioning has its own structure. A question requires three things: that which is asked about, that which is interrogated, and finally, that which it is hoping to find out.[2] For example, in a police investigation, a detective is inquiring into a robbery. She is therefore asking about the robbery. She interrogates a passer-by, who witnessed the events in question. This witness is that which is being interrogated. What the detective is seeking, what she is hoping to find out, is how the robbery took place, who was involved and so forth. In order to ask about the robbery she already has to have a clue that something like a robbery has taken place and she must therefore have some understanding of what a robbery is. She will need a preliminary understanding of what has occurred and what a robbery is in order to start the investigation. She will need the witness or some other clue in order to conduct the interrogation. Finally, she will need to have an idea of what she hopes to find out from the witness and thus where the investigation is going. The detective can only conduct this investigation if she is already open to what has taken place, what clues are present that can be interrogated and where she is going. She does not have a precise understanding of them from the start, but they must already be 'there' for her if she is to begin.

The structure that belongs to interrogation and questioning turns out to be a clue as to how anything is 'there' for us, not only when we are undertaking specific inquiries into this or that thing, but in the very way we exist at all. We are beings that are always questioning what it means for things to be, even if we do not explicitly formulate the question. In investigating the robbery, we rely on a preliminary understanding of the event that took place and seek to elaborate that understanding. Dasein is a being that can ask what Heidegger calls in *Being and Time* the question of the meaning of being, that is, of what it means for anything to be. In doing so we draw ourselves into question, because we are the beings that have some understanding of being. Questioning ourselves on our own understanding of being does not entail that we are utterly at a loss as to who we are or what it is for anything to be. On the contrary, to question ourselves we must have some idea of who we are, just as the detective must have some idea of what a robbery is in order to investigate it. Nor does questioning simply entail developing a 'questioning attitude'. There is no real questioning unless we are actually trying to come to a better understanding of that which is asked about. This is how we open up the 'there' that belongs to each of us and in which anything at all appears.

## ii. HERMENEUTICS, PHILOSOPHY AND ONTOLOGICAL DIFFERENCE

If questioning always begins from where we are and Dasein can question its own being because it is open to where it is, such questioning would seem to be torn between two claims. On the one hand, Dasein is 'there', in a unique situation in its historical and personal particularity. As Heidegger puts it, Dasein is 'in each case mine'.[3] On the other hand, what we are trying to understand in philosophy is surely the universal character of this 'there' that belongs to all. In the analysis outlined above Heidegger claims that *each and every* questioning has a certain structure. So the 'there' put into question does not seem to be unique and particular, but open to everyone at all times. Is it possible to give an account of how Dasein exists as being 'there', that is both philosophical and open to historical and personal particularity?

In a lecture course from 1923, *Ontology – The Hermeneutics of Facticity*, Heidegger identifies precisely this difficulty as comprising the situation in which he finds himself as a philosopher at that time. It is a situation that in many respects we are still faced with. He begins by identifying two prevalent tendencies in self-interpretation. First, 'historical consciousness' moves around between times and cultures making particular comparisons here and there, but understanding each to have a unified style which is in principle equal to all the others.[4] We are interested in each and every kind of cultural and historical form for the sake of developing a morphology or taxonomy of forms and giving each its due. The second form of thought, philosophy, understands itself as engaged in a kind of universal classification and sees itself as building up an objective metaphysics free from historical contingency.[5] Such a philosophy may end up trying to think through a temporal and historical situation and even think of itself as fundamentally concerned with this, but it will do so in terms of generalities which share a common root with those employed by historical consciousness.

Both of these forms of thought actually end up subjecting the situation that Dasein opens up for itself to generalities. Heidegger, on the other hand, hopes to develop a more adequate way of thinking about ourselves as self-questioning and self-interpreting beings. That way of thinking is what he called at this time the *hermeneutics of facticity*. Hermeneutics is frequently used to mean a theory or doctrine of interpretation. However, Heidegger argues that there is a much more fundamental role for hermeneutics in philosophy than might be imagined. It is not just that it can help us to re-appraise philosophical texts from the past and interpret them in the proper manner. If Dasein's life fundamentally involves self-interpretation, then as a practice of interpretation, that life will itself be hermeneutic. Clearly that does not mean that everyone has a well-formed doctrine about what interpretation is and how it should proceed. It means that: 'In hermeneutics what is developed for Dasein is a possibility of its becoming and being for itself in the manner of an *understanding* of itself.'[6]

The choice between trying to develop a historically particular understanding of ourselves and trying to develop a universal understanding that applies 'everywhere and always' is a false dilemma. The hermeneutics by which Dasein comes to an understanding of itself is not something that can be worked through to the end and then applied, either to particular cases or universally. Dasein holds itself in question and thus comes to an understanding of itself. What Heidegger thinks is required is not that we bring this questioning to an end so that we have some ready-made categories that can be applied to life. Rather, we need to hold ourselves in the question and make our questioning of ourselves as intense and explicit as possible. If philosophy is a complete framework for understanding that we try to apply to life from the outside, whether specifically or universally, then, 'hermeneutics is not philosophy at all, but in fact something preliminary that runs in advance of it.'[7] Hermeneutics in Heidegger's sense is *contemporary* with the self-questioning life of Dasein, not in the sense that it needs to be 'topical' or 'relevant to today', but in the sense that it is in time with the questioning and interpreting of our own lives. It shares the particular time in which Dasein lives and is coming to an understanding of itself.

Does this mean that Heidegger has abandoned philosophy altogether? It certainly means that his aim is not to elaborate 'a philosophy' that can be applied to things or to our own lives after the fact. For him there is no question of making philosophy 'relevant' to life, not because it has to remain hopelessly divorced from life, but because we are not trying to step outside of life so as to view it from some supposedly objective standpoint. We are trying to achieve the intensification and making explicit of the questioning and interpretation of ourselves that is our existence. Nevertheless, Heidegger is clear that a difference can be maintained between the

basic ways of being that belong to Dasein and the way that it actually lives its life in each case. He formalizes this difference in *Being
and Time* by introducing the terms 'existentiell' and 'existential'.[8]
The former refers to the interpretation of Dasein's life that gets
worked out in the living itself, its particular modes of existence.
Dasein understands itself in each case as having a profession, being
a certain kind of person and so forth. The latter refers to the understanding that Dasein develops of its own interpretative life, the
basic possibilities that allow it to come to such self-understanding.
So for Heidegger there is a difference between philosophical concepts and their particular concrete instantiations, but it is not a
difference between universally applicable generalizations and more
localized particular trends. It is a difference that is maintained in
the interpretation itself between the basic possibilities that belong
to a kind of being and how those possibilities are actualized in each
case.

Heidegger's philosophy investigates the 'existential' structures of
Dasein's existence. The concepts that it develops in doing so are a
little like what Kant had called 'transcendental' concepts. Those are
concepts that tell us not how things actually are in each case but
what the 'conditions of the possibility' of those things are. Heidegger
thought that we must develop transcendental reflection on our own
existence. However, since Dasein's existence is fundamentally the
interpretation of itself, our thought cannot simply run in one direction, back towards a characterization of the basic conditions of
that existence. It must also understand those conditions in terms of
the ways that it actually lives them out in its own life. A philosophical *existentiale* (category of existence) is born out of the existence
of Dasein as it lives out its own *existentiell* interpretation of itself.
On the other hand, these *existentiales* describe the very possibility
of Dasein's *existentiell* life and so are 'prior' to any particular living
out of that life. The temptation is to think of philosophical understanding as moving in one direction only, but Heidegger is quite
clear that what is called for in philosophical understanding is a
movement between the existential and existentiell, back and forth
movement between the conditions of possible existence and the
actual ways in which Dasein exists. An 'existentiale' is a special
kind of category, a basic concept that can describe the basic
possibilities of Dasein's existence. Yet they mean nothing if they
are not lived out. As Heidegger claims in an early lecture course,

*Phenomenological Interpretations of Aristotle*, 'Categories can be understood only insofar as factical life itself is compelled to interpretation.'[9] So a transcendental understanding of what is possible in any life must also be each life's own understanding of what those transcendental possibilities mean for it.

The difference between the existential and existentiell applies to our own existence. It is not a distinction between two different kinds of beings. Rather, it is a difference between what we might call distinct moments in Dasein's self-interpretation. Dasein can think of itself in terms of this difference, but it also maintains this difference in its understanding of anything at all. Dasein can understand 'ontologically' because it can understand the being of beings, that is, try to understand the basic possibilities of their being. At the same time it understands them 'ontically', with regard to what it actually is in each case. Since it is Dasein that can understand beings in their basic possibility and as what they actually are, it is Dasein that maintains what Heidegger comes to call an 'ontological difference' between beings and their being. In fact, it is precisely the kind of being that we are that we exist between the ontological and the ontic, since our questioning interpretations move in a 'relatedness backwards and forwards' between ontological and ontic understanding.[10] We do this because we are beings that seek to understand our own being and at the same time what it means for anything to be. So Dasein is not just a being that seeks to understand itself, but is a being that can ask the 'question of being', that is, it can interpret the meaning of being itself. There is no ontological difference without the Dasein that has an understanding of itself along with whatever it is trying to understand. This is the most important reason that Dasein is the starting point for any philosophical inquiry. In existing it maintains a difference between beings and their being, thus, 'providing the ontico-ontological condition for the possibility of any ontologies'.[11] If we want to understand the being of anything at all we must at the same time understand ourselves as the beings that can distinguish between the basic possibilities of being and their actual instantiations as beings.

### iii. THE FACTS OF LIFE

Heidegger did not understand Dasein's life as resting upon certain facts that then come to be interpreted by it. The fundamental fact about our lives is that we have an understanding of what can be and that in living we are elaborating that understanding: 'Interpreting is a being which belongs to the being of factical life itself.'[12] This may seem somewhat absurd. What then becomes of the 'facts' that seem so clearly to be beyond my control? Is Heidegger claiming that we can simply be whatever we want to be? Are there not certain brute facts that we cannot escape from and that are not open to interpretation at all, but simply are what they are? Heidegger's claim is that interpretation is primary, not that it is exempt from dealing with such facts. Our way of living is a 'factical life' involving a 'hermeneutics of facticity' precisely because by living out these lives as a questioning and interpretation of ourselves we reveal what is possible for us, what we can do and what we are unable to do.

This situation in which we all find ourselves is what Heidegger calls in *Being and Time* thrownness: 'The expression "thrownness" is meant to suggest *the facticity of being delivered over*.'[13] We never present ourselves with a completely blank canvas of possibilities, we always find ourselves thrown into circumstances that are not entirely of our own making. However, on the other hand, the facticity of our lives is never something that simply presents itself as the way things are, it is never the kind of 'brute fact' that belongs to things that we can simply observe as being the case. For example, I can simply observe that a box in front of me is of a certain size. In the same way I can simply observe that somebody is of average height. This is what Heidegger calls 'factuality', something that he sharply distinguishes from the facticity that belongs to Dasein's existence. Facticity is what that height actually means to the Dasein thrown into this situation. It is a question of the possibilities that are opened up and closed off to this Dasein. The facticity of a Dasein's height might include being disadvantageously short to play basketball. The so-called 'brute facts' reveal themselves as more or less mobile in terms of Dasein's self-understanding, for example, its wanting to play basketball well. In pursuing this possibility it makes its height an issue for itself. It can try to learn to play in such a way that its height is not disadvantageous. It may even find possible tactics for play that are not open to taller players. In the end, however, it may be that none of this is helpful and that this Dasein must revise its whole understanding of itself as a potentially good player. Then its height will weigh upon it as something that cannot be changed, but only in the light of its wanting to be a good player, not as a simple matter of fact.

What anchors or mobilizes the facts of any situation into which Dasein is thrown is thus the understanding of itself that it is working out as it lives. The facts of life are recalcitrant and immobile to the extent we have, as we all have to one extent or another, a received understanding of ourselves that comes to us from our earlier selves and from others. Sometimes there is a tendency to think that it is our embodiment that presents us with the most recalcitrant and immobile facts. We may feel that while we can replace, alter or escape anything else in our situation, our bodies are always there and cannot be 'escaped'. It is always as embodied that I am thrown into a situation. However, this does not mean that the facticity that arises from being thrown into a situation as embodied is not open to question. Being open to question does not mean that we can simply deny what is revealed to us as thrown into our situation. Rather, it means that we only work out what the facts mean, what can and cannot be done with them and about them, in living out a situation and that might involve very significant changes in our own embodiment.

Does Heidegger's concept of thrownness and of facticity thus give us an unproblematic way of understanding Dasein's embodiment? Heidegger is often accused of thinking of Dasein as a primarily disembodied entity and of failing to provide a detailed analysis of how it is embodied. For example, he writes of Dasein in gender neutral terms, as 'it' instead of 'he' or 'she'. Does this mean that Dasein has no gender or sex? Does it mean that it has no sexuality? If so, then it would seem to be very implausible to claim that such a being is the being that we ourselves are. Surely these are some of the most significant 'facts' about our own existence, so that an analysis which leaves them to one side would not only be incomplete but fundamentally distorted.

In 1928 Heidegger responded to this kind of concern with the analysis presented in *Being and Time* by claiming that the problem must be addressed in terms a certain kind of 'neutrality' of that analysis: 'The peculiar *neutrality* of the term "Dasein" is essential, because the interpretation of this being must be carried out prior to every factual concretion. This neutrality also indicates that Dasein is neither of the two sexes.'[14] However, he goes on to claim that this neutrality should not be seen as the abstraction away from concretely embodied existence. Rather, it is meant to be an interpretation that allows us to see how it is possible that each of us *is* concretely embodied in the way that we are: 'Neutral Dasein is never what exists: Dasein exists in each case only in its factical concretion. But neutral Dasein is indeed the primal source of intrinsic possibility that springs up in every existence and makes it intrinsically possible.'[15] The interpretation of Dasein is not meant to give us the essential facts about our existence by taking away all that seems inessential and contingent and leaving us with only the bare minimum. On the contrary, it is supposed to give us an analysis of how this being exists that includes *all* of the potential variety of its concrete particularity: 'As such, Dasein harbors the intrinsic possibility for being factically dispersed into bodiliness and thus into sexuality.'[16] What is held open here is not whether or not Dasein is 'dispersed' into bodiliness and sexuality, but how that occurs in each case and how that Dasein understands itself in its embodiment and sexuality.

Each Dasein is thrown into its life as embodied. That life includes all of the complex and interrelated 'facts' that make up its embodiment. When Heidegger says that his interpretation of Dasein is 'carried out prior to every factual concretion', it is not that there could be a point in life at which none of these facts were in place so that Dasein actually exists as neutral. Rather, we discover certain facts and come to an understanding of what they mean for us within the ongoing interpretation that is our existence. What the ontological interpretation of Dasein is supposed to achieve is an analysis not of one particular kind of concrete existence or another, but of the kind of being that can have all of the different 'ontic' embodiments that we have had, do have and that we can have. The 'neutrality' of the analysis of Dasein has the effect not of saying that we actually exist as disembodied, but that our embodiment along with every aspect of the situation into which we are thrown is not restricted to the forms and formulations that are already in place but is open to question.[17] Not that any Dasein thrown into a situation can simply throw off that situation all at once and, for example, utterly alter its embodiment at will. Often as we live out certain possibilities, we will uncover facts that are recalcitrant to our will. Yet their recalcitrance is not held within themselves as facts, but come to light within a particular understanding of the whole of Dasein's life. Heidegger's claim is not that there are no facts of life, but insofar as they are facts *of life* they are revealed not simply as bare facts, but in the questioning and interpreting of what is possible for it that characterizes 'factical life'.

## iv. MORE OR LESS HUMAN

Why does Heidegger tend to resist calling the being which we ourselves are 'human'? One reason is that we generally have all sorts of ideas as to what it is to be a human being. Everyone knows that human beings are given the name *Homo sapiens* in biological taxonomy. We are the kind of human that is distinguished by *thinking*, while our biological ancestors such as *Homo erectus* or *Homo habalis* were distinguished by standing erect or being skilled as craftsmen. All of this draws upon and feeds into a long tradition that informs both our ordinary everyday understanding of ourselves and our attempts at getting clear about ourselves philosophically. Heidegger identifies two central strands to this tradition, which he claims still govern our self-understanding, even if only covertly.[18] First, there is the definition of man in the ancient Greek philosophical tradition as *zōon logon echon*, the animal which has *logos*. This is then translated into Latin as *animal rationale*, the rational animal, the animal that has rationality as its defining feature. We are indisputably animals, but we are animals which are endowed with a 'special ability' that lifts us out of our animality. Precisely what this basic animality or the special ability of rationality amounts to is often left undetermined. This is one reason why Heidegger ceases to use the term 'life' to designate the existence of Dasein, because it is 'never to be defined ontologically by regarding it as life (in an ontologically indefinite manner) plus something else.'[19] Secondly, there is the religious, and for Heidegger specifically Christian, tradition that understands man as the creation of God. If we recall the creation story of Genesis this occurs by fashioning man from the earth and then breathing spirit, the breath of life, into him. Man is transcendent, because he is *more* than an intelligent animal, but again, how this *more* is unified in one kind of being with what is less is left undetermined.

A central feature of both of these traditions is that they understand a human being as a kind of conglomeration of properties. On the one hand, we understand ourselves as animals with particular abilities. Even if we develop a complex understanding of what those abilities are that relates them to our evolutionary history, we are still thinking of ourselves in basically the same way. On the other hand, we can say that we are body, soul and spirit united. Even if we develop a complex way of thinking about what is involved in body, soul and spirit we are still thinking of ourselves as a conglomeration of these three features. What we do not properly understand is how all of the properties or abilities are unified in us and what the basic character of our existence is that allows them to be so unified. However much detail we are able to provide about precisely what the abilities are that we have and why we have come to have them, that will not answer the question of what it means to be a being that can exist in the way we do with those abilities or properties, and potentially others. We are beings that can ask that question of ourselves and we do so by understanding possibilities as being open to us: 'In each case Dasein *is* its possibility, and it "has" this possibility, but not just as a property [. . .]'[20] We exist as the living out of our possibilities. Yet the meaning of any ability that I am able to exercise is not just a question of what I do with it, but also of what I could do but do not. It is also a question of what I could never do and what I might be able to do. Furthermore, my abilities make sense in terms of what I have been able to do but cannot do any longer or cannot do for the moment, in terms of what others can do and I cannot, and so forth. What Dasein's abilities mean for it, in its existence as coming to understand itself, is never just a question of what it has done and will do, but also a question of what was, is and will be open to it. So its entire range of possibilities gives sense to each of its abilities and actions.

This means that we must radically rethink the kind of being that we are. We are not beings that have certain properties and abilities, some of which are essential and some of which are inessential. What is involved in existing as Dasein is not the possession of any particular ability or set of abilities, but the understanding of those abilities in terms of the entire range of its possibilities. So existing as Dasein does not mean that we are not human beings, in whatever way we might wish to define what is essential to being human. It is rather that because we exist as Dasein, being human and having whatever properties or abilities that involves, means something to us. What it means to us does not have to be formulated in an explicit definition and is usually not open to definition aside from some very specific purposes, because it involves an assumed and extremely complex way of understanding the various possibilities that are open to ourselves and others. For the most part any determinate definition of a human being that is formulated will serve certain specific purposes, but will be unable to capture the range of things that being human means to us. That is why formulating a definition can be so dangerous, unless it is done with a view not only to what that definition is intended to do, but what it might mean when taken up in quite different circumstances. Even the most vague notion of what it means to be human can mean a great deal to us in terms of who we understand ourselves to be. So being Dasein is a pre-requisite for understanding ourselves as human beings in any kind of vague and implicit way or with a precise and explicit definition, all of which are specific possibilities for Dasein.

Are there not other beings, other than those traditionally designated as human beings, that exist as Dasein? In particular, are there not other living beings that can 'question' in Heidegger's sense, be 'there' and understand their own possibilities? This is a question that is very much on the periphery of *Being and Time*. The real difficulty comes with trying to understand how living beings are in what we call their 'environment'. This is also the question that Heidegger thinks must be the first that we ask when we try to understand how Dasein exists, as we shall see in the following chapter. In lectures before *Being and Time*, Heidegger suggests that living beings are open to their world and are therefore 'there' as Dasein, even if the world they are open to may not be very complex:

Every living creature has its environing world not as something extant next to it but as something that is there [*da ist*] for it as disclosed, uncovered. For a primitive animal, the world can be very simple. But life and its world are never two things side by side; rather, life "has" its world.[21]

A living being does not just stand there next to its environment, nor does it only come into contact with its environment when something impinges on it or when it ingests something from it. A living being is open to its environment from the start, which is why things can impinge on it. In a lecture course from 1924, Heidegger also calls all living beings Dasein, and designates their kind of being as 'being-in-the-world', the very kind of being that he attributes to that being that 'we ourselves are' in *Being and Time*: 'Life is being-in-a-world. Animals and humans are not at hand next to one another, but are with one another, and (in the case of humans) they express themselves reciprocally.'[22] However, Heidegger thinks that this 'reciprocal expression' that comes with speaking, is not for us an added extra but the very 'being-context' in which certain living beings live, so that in sharing a world with other living beings we only do so in this kind of reciprocity with those who speak.

Heidegger returns to this problem in earnest in an important lecture course from 1929/30, *The Fundamental Concepts of Metaphysics: World, Finitude, Solitude*, where he makes a sustained attempt to work out how living beings are in their surrounding environment. Now he claims that we cannot fully address this question in terms of the simplicity and complexity of the surrounding world that is 'there' for a living being. Some may be relatively simple and some may be very complex. Ultimately, it is a question of trying to see the *way* in which living beings are in their surroundings, regardless of complexity. At first Heidegger seems to be quite dogmatic about this, beginning with three theses: the stone is worldless; the animal is poor in world; man is world-forming.[23] However, as he progresses it becomes clear that the purpose of this starting point is not to make dogmatic assertions about what living beings are and what they can and cannot do. Rather, it is to open up the problem of characterizing precisely how living beings have access to what surrounds them, a concern that brings with it the problem of how we who are trying to make that characterization have access to their way of being open. We encounter animals, and indeed all living beings, in a world and see that they inhabit their surroundings in a way which stones do not. The problem is with giving an account of that inhabiting of an environment which does not simply project onto other animals the way that we inhabit our own world. As human beings we are never simply faced with other living beings, but we are transposed into their environments:

> The difficulty of the problem lies in the fact that in our questioning we always inevitably interpret the poverty in world and the particular encirclement proper to the animal in such a way that we end up talking as if that which the animal relates to and the manner in which it does so were some being, and as if the relation involved were an ontological relation that is manifest to the

animal. The fact that this is not the case forces us to claim that the *essence of life can become accessible to us only if we consider it in a deconstructive* [abbauenden] *fashion*. But this does not mean that life represents something inferior or some kind of lower level in comparison to human Dasein. On the contrary, life is a domain which possesses a wealth of openness with which the human world may have nothing to compare.[24]

This passage begins to show why a phenomenological characterization of living beings is so difficult. Unlike many philosophical accounts that attempt to 'rank' living beings in terms of their abilities, Heidegger argues that such a procedure is entirely beside the point. What we need to do is to try to characterize the basic way in which living beings have any capacities that they do have and how this allows them access to what surrounds them. It is the way that living beings have access to their environment that makes them living beings in the first place. Heidegger develops the concept of 'captivation' within an encircling ring to try to understand the environment of living beings. The point is not that living beings are caught within a rigid and inflexible set of relations to what surrounds them.[25] Rather, the thought is that living beings are absorbed in behavior towards what surrounds them. This 'ring' of possibility allows for their behavior, but in so behaving they are not related to what makes their behavior possible. It is not an ontological relation because it does not form an understanding of its own openness. Yet because human Dasein does form such an understanding in its very openness to what is there for it, including living beings, it is, in a sense, bound to misunderstand beings that do not. While we would have no access to them whatsoever without some understanding of them and it is necessary to try to make that understanding as adequate to the phenomena as possible, that does not mean that by developing these concepts Heidegger thinks he has captured how living beings are in their environments once and for all. It remains an ongoing question that requires us to engage with our own self-understanding and how things are 'there' for us, so as to see how this informs and misinforms our apprehension of the way other living beings are open or closed to what surrounds them and how we may be open or closed to those other ways of living. Such ongoing questioning is precisely what makes up Dasein's way of living and engaging with what surrounds it.

# CHAPTER 3

# WORLD: THE EVENT OF MEANING

Meaning is a tool – a means. Absolute meaning would be means and end at the same time. Thus every thing is *itself the means* whereby we come to know it – to experience it or have an effect on it.

*Logological Fragments* I, 72

Philosophers can often be found thinking about a difficult and long-standing problem: the problem of the 'external world'. If we ask what exactly the world is supposed to be *external to* we can see that the presupposition here is that there is something or somewhere internal, such that the whole world is external to it. This inside could not be a spatial inside, in the way that a table can be in a room or tea can be in a cup, or the brain in the skull. A being that is internal in a way that the whole world is exterior to it has somehow ceased to be inside the world at all. It is what modern philosophy calls the *ego* or *subject*. It is a being that knows itself perfectly well, 'inside out' we might say, but has a constant need to find and prove to itself that there is a world that it inhabits.

The entire way in which the problem of world is set up and the consequent way in which we understand ourselves as subjects in the modern world is, for Heidegger, an enormous mistake. Responding to Kant's claim to have provided a proof that there is an external world, which has been scandalously left unaccomplished, Heidegger retorts: 'The "scandal of philosophy" is not that the proof has yet to be given, but that *such proofs are expected and attempted again and again.*'[1] The problem of the 'external world' is a problem that cannot find a solution because it is a wholly artificial problem. The problem arises when we fail to adequately characterize the phenomenon of world itself. The difficulty is not that of connecting the world up with something extra-worldy, but how to understand the world in the first place. When we present the problem of world as one of connecting up the world with something other than the world, then we have no chance of penetrating into the real difficulty, because we have already assumed an understanding of the world as one thing or set of things that can be connected up to something else. An adequate characterization of the world will not have to be supplemented by an understanding of ourselves, that is our 'Dasein', as outside but connected to the world, or as one particular kind of thing in the world. Dasein is not some being that is outside the world and needs to be connected up to it, but a being that has the character of 'being-in-the-world'. There is no problem of the external world, there is only the problem of characterizing how Dasein is there in the world.

### i. TACKLING THE WORLD AROUND US

Heidegger tried again and again throughout his philosophical career to provide an adequate characterization of the world and how it is that Dasein is in the world. In *Being and Time* he distinguishes four ways in which the word 'world' can be used. First, world can mean all the things that there are collected together. Second, it can mean an ontological understanding of those things. The example given is of the 'world of the mathematician', which embraces all the possible objects of mathematics and in doing so must have developed at least some understanding of what a mathematical object is. Third, there is a quite different sense of world, which is the world that each particular Dasein inhabits, that might include the 'world of the mathematician', but is not simply that world. Finally, we can develop an ontological understanding of the *worldhood* of this world, the character of the world itself that Dasein exists in.[2] We tend to think of the world as the complete collection of objects. The world can be encountered in this way, but Heidegger's claim is that this is not the primary way in which the world is encountered. When we do encounter the world as a complete collection of objects, then that is the result of something which has taken place in the world that Dasein inhabits, something that will have to be characterized as part of the analysis of how Dasein is in the world.

Dasein is not one thing among others in the world. It is not like water in a glass or garments in a cupboard.[3] When we say that somebody is in a room, we mean that they have a bodily location within that room. But when Heidegger says that Dasein is *in* the world he means that we are always 'out there' in a particular way in that world. I may have a bodily location in the room, but to be in the room in this sense would mean to be encountering things and people in the room, perhaps doing some work in the room, perhaps appreciating the design of the room. I might be located in the room and yet not in the room in this sense. I might be entirely absorbed in my own body, perhaps if I am ill or doing an exercise in which I am focused on the body. Alternatively I might be located in the room and yet be outside that room. I might be daydreaming that I am outside doing something else, planning what I am going to do later when I have left the room, or remembering something that occurred before I entered the room. It is because of this that we often find that someone is 'elsewhere' even when they are located in the room right next to us. Dasein can be there in its own body, in the room around it, or outside somewhere else, all while maintaining the same location. Dasein is in the world in each case, even when it is concerned only with its own body, because that body is itself within its world.

In *Being and Time* Heidegger chooses to begin his characterization of the world and how Dasein inhabits that world by concentrating on how we encounter the world on an everyday basis. The way in which we inhabit the world is primarily as an environment, so the analysis of worldhood begins with an analysis of environmentality. Everything that we encounter in our everyday dealings with the environment is characterized by Heidegger as 'equipment'. The first crucial characteristic of equipment is that it is primarily and before all else something directed towards something. Equipment has the character of being 'in-order-to'.[4] A pen is there in order to write, a knife in order to cut, a train in order to travel. That does not mean that in our usual dealings with the pen, we find it lying around and then decide to use it to write. Rather, it has been assigned this 'in-order-to' already. It may be a pen that I use every day to write. I do not think about it, but simply pick it up and start writing. It may be that I'm looking around for something to write with and then I find this pen, perfect for the job. It is not that I find the pen and then ask myself what sort of thing it might be good for.

I see it immediately as something with which I can write. As I look around things present themselves as facilitating this 'in-order-to' of writing or not. There is thus a particular kind of looking that belongs to environmental dealings with equipment, which is not simply looking at an object, but rather this 'looking around', or 'circumspection', in which we see things in terms of an 'in-order-to' do this or that.[5] The things we encounter are already subordinated to this 'in-order-to', but that does not mean that this character belongs to them like one of their properties, such as being blue. A Dasein who is not engaged in writing at all may encounter the pen. It may be looking around for something to help hook out its keys that have fallen behind a cupboard. Everything about the pen will then appear in terms of whether or not it will achieve this aim.

The kind of being that belongs to 'equipment' Heidegger calls the 'ready-to-hand',[6] a term he coins to contrast with the 'present-at-hand'. While being 'present-at-hand' in German usually just means that something is in some way there, Heidegger makes it into a particular way of being that belongs to objects that are simply there before us. What is 'ready-to-hand' by contrast is not just lying before us, but is there 'in-order-to' do something.

We encounter our environment by 'looking around', and find equipment as 'in-order-to' do this or that. A second important characteristic of equipment is that we do not encounter it primarily in isolated items or pieces: 'Taken strictly, there "is" no such thing as *an* [item of] equipment.'[7] We may say of a certain object that it is a 'piece' of equipment, but what we usually mean is that it has been produced to fulfil a particular role in a certain project. Nevertheless, as an isolated piece of equipment it could not actually fulfil that role. Even the simplest activity requires all sorts of equipment that we do not usually consider, but take for granted. Writing to a friend involves pen, ink, table and chair. That is what we usually think of as the equipment. Yet it also involves my fingers, arm, eyes, muscles and nervous system. It involves a postal system, with all of the transport and people involved in the transport. All of this is 'equipment' in Heidegger's sense and it is equipment because it has the character of being 'involved' with all the rest. The whole of the involvement in which everything refers onwards beyond itself is what Heidegger calls an 'equipmental whole'.[8]

A common English term that we might employ to show how Heidegger understands the everyday environment of equipment is 'tackle'. Tackle is both a noun meaning 'gear or equipment' and a verb 'to tackle', which has the sense of dealing with or handling something. As a verb it can mean to tackle a particular thing, such as tackling someone on the sportsfield. But what we are tackling is primarily a whole circumstance, to deal with that situation and to handle it in one way or another. One tackles someone in sport as part of tackling a whole circumstance that one finds oneself in on the field. There is no point in tackling some particular thing if that action is not directed towards one's wider circumstances. The history of the term 'tackle' records that when the noun was first used as a verb it meant 'to entangle or involve'. In this term we have thus compressed the ontological characteristics of what Heidegger calls equipment. In tackling its surroundings, the tackle that is ready-to-hand for Dasein is entangled and involved as a whole. We can take fishing tackle as an example. There is the obvious sense in which bait is no good without a hook to put it on and a line to tie the hook to. A box of fishing hooks is not on its own fishing tackle, but it is likely to be involved in fishing tackle. A rod and a net are also likely to be part of the tackle. Is that all that makes up the tackle? We are only able to think this way because of a rather narrow view of what is involved in going fishing. Again, this is what we usually think of as 'the tackle', all the items we can buy in a tackle shop. What is really involved in going fishing is much more. Almost everything involved in the tackle as a whole is taken for granted. The tackle involves a body of water, be it a river, lake or sea. Unless this is 'fishing' in the sense of having a pleasant day by the river, the tackle will also crucially involve fish. It will involve everything that allows the fish to be there, its food, its oxygen supply and so forth. Once we come to see that 'fishing tackle' is not simply confined to the box of hooks and bait, the rod and line, then it is very hard to see an end to this context of involvements. The fish requires a lake, river or sea, oxygenating plants, complex geological and climatic processes and cycles. All of this is 'involved' in the surrounding world of a Dasein that goes fishing. All of this and much more is involved in the whole of fishing tackle. The tackle does not just involve those items that we usually think of as tools or artificial things as opposed to natural things. Nature itself, in our everyday ways of tackling our environment, is involved in the tackle: 'The wood is a forest of timber, the mountain a quarry of rock; the river is water-power, the wind is wind in the sails.'[9] This is brought to the fore by one further meaning of the verb to tackle, 'to harness a horse'. Tackling the environment is thus not just a question of bringing our own effort to bear upon it, it can also involve harnessing the effort that nature and natural things provide.

This whole context of involvements is what Dasein takes for granted when it tackles its surroundings and it is also that with which it tackles its surroundings. Heidegger describes this context of involvements as that, 'on the basis of which and with respect to which', [*Woraufhin*] Dasein is able to encounter and tackle anything at all.[10] It is not the case that Dasein comes into the world and then goes about making things into tackle so that they become involved with one another. Rather, whenever it is in the world then that world is a world of involved tackle that it relies upon and handles in one way or another. The involved whole on the basis of which and with respect to which we tackle the world around us is further characterized by Heidegger as 'significance'.[11] The relational whole is one in which everything signifies, in the sense of pointing onwards within the whole. For example, a cloud signifies rain, rain signifies that I should bring my umbrella and so forth. The whole context in which things signify one another in this manner, the 'equipmental whole', is at the same time a 'referential whole'.[12] It would be easy to misunderstand what Heidegger is trying to point us towards here if we assume that using things as tools and using them as signs are simply certain ways of tackling the world that Dasein adopts once it is faced with an environment and a situation that it must tackle. What we call using something as a tool or piece of equipment, adapting something to be used as a tool or producing a tool is possible because Dasein is already in an equipmental whole. I can only adapt a stick and a pin to become fishing tackle, because the whole understanding of my surroundings as somewhere that one can go fishing is already in place. Similarly Dasein can adapt things to use as 'signs', which are very particular kinds of equipment. Signs can be more or less arbitrary, as is made clear by Heidegger's own example of a knot in a handkerchief, which can be used to signify more or less anything.[13] There are signs that I can establish for myself and there are signs that already have an established meaning. However, all of this takes place within a 'referential whole' that is already in place whenever Dasein comes to signify anything with anything else and which coincides with Dasein's being in a world at all. I can only use the knotted handkerchief to remind me to visit the dentist, if there is a whole significant context in place involving dentists and bad teeth and what it will mean if I do not go. What gives the sign its peculiar character is that it is able to indicate the referential whole, and it is that whole which gives sense to the knot or perhaps to a note on a calendar that simply reads 'dentist'.[14] The whole involvement of tackle is the assumed basis upon which Dasein can use tools to tackle anything. The referential whole of significations is also the assumed basis upon which Dasein can use anything as a sign, and the sign points us towards the whole in which circumstances are to be tackled. The 'worldhood' of the world is the whole within which Dasein can tackle its environment and use signs to point out significant circumstances.

## ii. ENVIRONMENTAL BREAKDOWN AND RECOVERY

The involved and referential whole is in place whenever Dasein is in the world. It is the way that Dasein inhabits the world and is able to encounter anything within that world. Yet this turns out to be quite problematic. If Dasein is caught up in the whole of its surroundings, where there are primarily no items of equipment but only the whole involved tackle of the ready-to-hand by means of which it handles and negotiates its surroundings, how is it that any part of this whole ever shows up within this world? When things are going well our attention is drawn neither to the whole context of involvements, 'the referential whole', nor to any particular thing. What is peculiar about the 'ready-to-hand', is that when it is genuinely ready-to-hand it 'withdraws'.[15] So how is it that anything ever makes an appearance from out of this whole contexture of involvements? How do *phenomena* show themselves in our everyday surrounding environment?

The answer is to be found in the disruption of the smooth running of the whole. This does not happen only occasionally, but is something that is constantly taking place, drawing out things from the referential whole and then allowing them to fall back into it. In *Being and Time* Heidegger distinguishes three such occurrences. The ready-to-hand becomes *'conspicuous'* if equipment breaks or becomes unusable in some way.[16] The fishing line might break when I hook a huge carp. The line becomes conspicuous and I see for the first time that it is not strong enough. However, I am probably already ahead of the game and just as the line announces its presence I am busy repairing it or replacing it with something more suitable. So the line will then fall back into the whole. In a more extreme case, something may announce itself by being completely absent and 'un-ready-to-hand', and then it becomes *obtrusive*.[17] I may have forgotten the line and left it at home. I can see the line sitting there uselessly in my drawer. Strangely, the line itself makes itself known precisely because it is not to hand and the worldly character of my environmental dealings is disrupted because I cannot easily fix the situation. Finally, things may be *obstinate* and refuse themselves as ready-to-hand.[18] Everything is in place, my line does not break, but the carp is simply too big and too strong for me to land. The presence of this huge and powerful fish nevertheless makes itself known as something which calls out to be tackled.

The result of this analysis is that the surrounding world of ready-to-hand tackle is seen to be always full of hitches. If it ever ran without a hitch then no 'items' of equipment would emerge and the character of the ready-to-hand itself would also remain concealed. It is only because there is breakdown in the connections of involvement and reference that the items themselves become apparent, together with the involved and referential character of the whole. When the fishing line breaks it emerges from the whole as an item of equipment, but the character of involvement that it had when all was going well also emerges. For much of the time equipment runs relatively smoothly. There are breakdowns and hitches in which the ready-to-hand becomes un-ready-to-hand, but these can be repaired or got around in one way or another so that they return to being ready-to-hand. There is also the possibility that what was ready-to-hand becomes just 'present-at-hand' for us, so that items are extracted from their involvement. One possibility is then that they become the objects of a theoretical study in which they are just looked at in their own right. However, they do not thereby entirely lose all connection to the whole from which they have emerged. We know that theoretical study is often undertaken with a view to putting things back into an equipmental whole that runs more smoothly than ever. It is important to notice that there is this continual change in the character of things in the world, in *how* they are. Tackle that was unnoticed and taken for granted breaks down. It may simply be fixed and returned to the involved whole, or it may prove more obstinate and present itself as useless junk, until it is repaired or put to some other use. Items and complex structures of items can also be extracted from the whole and theoretically studied. Their being-character is not fixed but changes with regard to how they are situated within the whole.

Since Heidegger worked out this analysis of the character of the surrounding world we have witnessed events that have led to a growing awareness of our environment. More and more frequently there have been no fish when we go fishing, they have been *obtrusively* absent; or they have been *conspicuously* small and sickly. It is not only the fish that we used to be able to take for granted that have announced themselves in this way. There are more and more breakdowns in the whole 'tackle' that we used to be able to take for granted: the seas, rivers, land and air. These events have given us a start, a shock, as the environment which we inhabit in our everyday lives announces itself with great urgency. What has announced itself is not just particular isolated items, such that we could fix the fish and get on with fishing as before, but the *involvement of things as a whole*. We see the fish are involved in plants, water, geological formations and so forth. Through an unprecedented breakdown the environmental whole has become present. Since it has become present in this way, we have developed a theoretical view of that environment, an environmental science that tries to take all of the involved connections into account and to aid environmental recovery. This science has proved to be extremely powerful in enabling us to overcome some aspects of the breakdown. Yet we understand that the artificial isolation of objects in the laboratory or in the field that allows us to fix our attention upon them, can only tell us so much. It can be positively misleading because it studies only isolated sets of involvements and then tries to patch them back together. In a sense the worldly character of the environment has come into view, but when we try to fix it before us we are in danger of missing it altogether. The involvement of one thing in another takes on a totally different character when it is fixed, for example, in the form of a 'food web' in which not only is each living being objectified, but the relations between them become further objects which serve to fix and glue them together. Even when the web is made into a dynamic simulated model, each involvement has to be isolated beforehand so that they can be set to work together to see what effects that produces. Because this can be such a powerful way to proceed, we develop a tendency to think that the only way to prevent further catastrophic breakdown is to *fix* the environment, in the interrelated senses of presenting it to ourselves as a system of isolable relations that we then try to ensure remain intact. What we thereby miss is that a genuinely ready-to-hand environment is not one that can be fixed in place in this way, but one which allows us to tackle each and every circumstance. It is a whole that can be allowed to recover when breakdown occurs and when it recovers in that way the involved whole becomes inconspicuous. According to Heidegger inhabiting an environment also entails that we are able to release beings into their involvement, that we are able to 'let-something-be-involved'.[19] If we try to make our surrounding world into a place where there is no such letting things be involved, then its way of being and at the same time our way of inhabiting it will be fundamentally altered. The environment may be divested of its character of being an involved whole and fixed into a system of isolable functions, at precisely the moment when we are being forced to acknowledge its significance as a whole.

### iii. OUR WORLD OWNS ITSELF

The tackle that Dasein relies upon and puts to use in its everyday surrounding world has the character of being 'in-order-to'.[20] The involved referential whole is directed in one way or another and has the character of 'towards-which'.[21] In the case of fishing, the hook is baited in order to attract the fish and everything is geared towards landing the fish. Nevertheless, that is not where the referential and involved whole comes to an end. The fish itself usually has the character of equipment. It may be eaten 'in-order-to' keep the Dasein who caught it nourished. Is that the end point of the whole? Again, it is something towards which things are geared, but it is not the final end in which all these actions are fulfilled. The body of Dasein itself becomes involved in the equipmental whole, it is relied upon and made use of in further concerns. Each and every product and achievement is taken up and directed onwards in this way. There does not seem to be any point at which these concerned dealings come finally to an end, so we are led to ask whether and how the whole itself can have any ultimate 'point' or meaning.

It is not in an isolable item or achievement that the whole surrounding world of involvements finds its end. Heidegger's own example involves hammering. Hammering is involved in making something fast, making something fast is involved in protection against bad weather and protection against bad weather is for the sake of sheltering Dasein. The whole of the surrounding world finds its end, its 'primary towards which', in that 'for the sake of which' this all takes place in the being of *Dasein*.[22] Yet recall that the purpose of this characterization of the surrounding world was precisely to try to uncover the kind of being that belongs to Dasein in its everyday being-in-the-world. The being whose way of being it is to bring about this whole is also the being for-the-sake-of-which the worldhood of the world takes place. How can a world that is primarily an involved whole in which everything is directed onwards be an end in itself? The problem is that Dasein gets caught up in the tackle and involved in its world. It assigns itself a role to play in the involvements of the surrounding world and is assigned such roles by others. This is what Heidegger designates as 'falling' into the world, a phenomenon that he devotes much time to analyzing. In a sense, as it tackles the world Dasein is constantly drawing itself into the tackle. This is not necessarily a bad thing, but rather it is an inevitable consequence of the equipmental character of the everyday surrounding world. The problem is that insofar as it is involved in the world Dasein understands itself as so involved, it is in danger of losing sight of its own character as that 'for-the-sake-of-which' the whole is there.

Perhaps the problem is that Heidegger has overemphasized the 'pragmatic' aspects of Dasein's being-in-the-world. Is this characterization of the everyday environment not unduly focused on 'the world of work'? Might one not argue that work is 'for-the-sake-of' times beyond and outside of this involvement, even when construed in the broadest sense? As the commentator Michel Haar put it in an attempt at internal critique of this analysis:

> When the "beauty of nature" strikes us in a shaft of sunlight, in the surprising diversity of forms and colors; when we see an animal playing; when we stand in a meadow in springtime; when we hear the ceaseless rumble of the waves, no equipmental relation is present which might subsequently be broken.[23]

These are surely not entirely unusual experiences. Neither do they necessarily take place in classically natural settings, but rather they can occur whenever and wherever Dasein is. The characterization

of the way that Dasein experiences and inhabits its everyday surrounding world seems to be incomplete without them. Is this not
a clue that might help us to understand how Dasein is something
'for-the-sake-of-which' every 'in-order-to' occurs?
In fact, in the 1919 lecture course in which he first dealt with the
problem of theoretical 'de-vivification', Heidegger had paid attention to precisely this kind of experience:

> In the morning I enter the study; the sun lies over the books, etc.,
> and I delight in this. Such delight is in no way an ought; 'delight-
> fulness' as such is not given to me in an ought-experience. I
> ought to work, I ought to take a walk: two motivations, two
> possible kinds of 'because' which do not reside in the delightful
> itself but presuppose it. There is, therefore, a kind of lived
> experience in which I take delight, in which the valuable as such
> is given.[24]

The delight that is experienced here is not in the first instance a
consequence of the sunlight facilitating going for a walk or working. Valuing takes place in such a way that I am taken by the sunlight in a 'worth-taking' and so delight in it. The valuing does not
take place in a subject and then get laid on top of the bare objective
sunlight, nor is it simply in the things and then picked up by
the subject. The experience of value is an event in which 'it values'
[es wertet] for me.[25] It is something that takes place before the subjective and the objective have been separated out. Later in the same
course Heidegger addresses the kind of environmental experience
that will form the basis for his analysis of the surrounding world
in *Being and Time*. In a lecture hall he experiences not isolated and
meaningless objects that he then has to give meaning to, but a
meaningful whole in which everything has a meaning with regard to
all the rest: 'Living in an environment, it signifies to me everywhere
and always, everything has the character of world. It is everywhere
the case that "it worlds" [es weltet], which is something different
from "it values" [es wertet].'[26]
Although in this early course Heidegger takes these two 'events'
as separable and regards their possible connection as a difficult
problem, he clearly does not see them as separable in the sense of
taking place separately. If the environment everywhere has the
character of 'worlding', of being, in Heidegger's later terms, an

involved whole, then the study or the lecture hall has that character even when he has not got down to work, but is simply experiencing the 'valuing' of the sunlight. Similarly, the 'valuing' of the taking as delightful, and presumably a whole range of other possible 'values', is also in play when he is at work in the involved whole. The two can be understood as formally separable aspects of the whole way in which the world is taken up and inhabited. A very similar distinction is made in *Being and Time* between the *disposition* and the *understanding* of Dasein, as we shall see in Chapters 5 and 6, but by then he has made it clearer that these cannot be treated as different experiences at all, but only as 'existentiales', categories designed to bring out the formal structure of the whole of Dasein's existence.

The way to understand the Dasein 'for-the-sake-of-which' the world takes place is thus not to look for special ends that interrupt the involved whole. Neither is it to look for a particular species of experience that takes place outside of that whole altogether. Rather, Heidegger's thought is that we can move from and through this analysis of everyday concernful dealings and all of the value-taking that goes along with them, to that which allows all of this to take place and allows Dasein's existence to be a whole, rather than a series of parts and experiences that are then somehow glued together. In a sense this will be both the beginning of the world, that is, what allows the world to be a world, and the end of the world, that is, that 'for-the-sake-of-which' it takes place. Yet as beginning and end it cannot be found somewhere outside of the world, but only by uncovering how the world comes about and takes place. Dasein can find the meaning of the world in itself, but doing so cannot involve turning away from the world and into itself, because its way of being is to be in the world. Rather, we need a more penetrating characterization of how it is that Dasein is in its world and thus how the world takes place and is open as 'there'. That is where Heidegger always took himself to be heading. In 1919 he gives us some idea of that way of being in and for a world, naming it the *event of appropriation* (*Ereignis*):

> Lived experience does not pass in front of me like a thing, but I appropriate [*er-eigne*] it to myself, and it appropriates itself according to its essence [. . .] Event of appropriation is not to be taken as if I appropriate the lived experience to myself from

outside or from anywhere else; 'outer' and 'inner' have as little meaning here as 'physical' and 'psychical'. The experiences are events of appropriation in so far as they live out of one's 'ownness', and life lives only in this way.[27]

It is in and through this event that the world with which we concern ourselves and get involved takes place. A few years later Heidegger will designate this event as 'care', and claim that we must understand care ontologically as time or temporality, which is the central claim of *Being and Time*.[28] In the 1930s the idea of an 'event of appropriation' is taken up once more and along with 'truth' becomes one of Heidegger's basic characterizations of how the world takes place as a significant whole. The philosophical problem of 'I' and 'world' has been completely transformed for Heidegger from the start and throughout all of these reworkings. It is not a question of how one thing called 'I' is connected up to another thing called 'world'. It is rather a question of experiencing the way in which this world takes place as an event through which all meaningfulness and valuation take place. It is an event that is our own and to which we reciprocally belong. To move in that direction we need to see in more detail how it is that Dasein loses contact with this event and in doing so loses itself in the world that it brings about.

# CHAPTER 4

# ANYONE AND EVERYONE

> Society is nothing but communal living – one indivisible thinking and feeling person. Each human being is a society in miniature.
>
> *Miscellaneous Observations,* 42

Just as it is an artificial problem to imagine ourselves as worldless minds somehow seeking to get into contact with a world, so it is an artificial problem to think of ourselves as primarily individuals who are seeking to come into contact with others. Neither the 'problem of the external world' nor the 'problem of other minds' can be solved on their own terms, because they misconstrue the fundamental way in which Dasein finds itself as being-in-the-world. The problem, in each case, turns out to be quite the opposite of that which these philosophical constructs imagine it to be. In the first case, Heidegger seeks to show that originally we are already in the world and that it is only very particular occurrences within that world that can disengage us from it. This world is also a world that we inhabit along with others right from the start. The problem is not primarily one of getting in touch with and understanding others, although that can become a problem that we have to face in particular circumstances. The primary problem is that of finding ourselves when we start out in the midst of a fundamentally shared world.

## i. ALREADY WITH OTHERS

Others do not primarily show up in the world like equipment or items, 'ready-to-hand' or 'present-at-hand'. However much others are instrumentalized or objectified, there is a lingering awareness that this is what has been done; that other Dasein are not simply a part of the equipmental context of the surrounding world, or objects arising from the breaking up of that context. Rather, we are with others primarily in the sense that we 'care-for' them.[1] This does not mean that we always care for others in the sense of liking them, wishing them well and trying to help them. That we can care for them in that sense is possible because we are there along with them in the world and we can see their concerns. It is precisely this way of being with others that also allows us to be completely uncaring in the usual sense. We can be so absorbed in our own concerns that we do not pay attention to theirs. Maliciousness is also only possible because we share a world in this way, since everyone cares how they are regarded by at least some others. We can also 'look out' for concerns of others with the intention of disrupting and frustrating them. Other Dasein have a world of concern, but that does not mean that their world is sealed off from mine. We share the same world, involving *our* concerns and disrupted concerns.

In his early lecture courses Heidegger sometimes speaks of three worlds: the surrounding-world, with-world and self-world.[2] This threefold division is best taken not as a classification of three separate worlds that are inhabited alongside one another, that is, as a world of equipment and things, a social world and an inner world of my own. Rather, it is an attempt to understand three different aspects or inflections of the one world that Dasein inhabits. How is it that all these three world inflections occur together? How do we exist within them and between them? In *The Basic Problems of Phenomenology*, a lecture course from 1927, Heidegger tried to show how this can be the case. He explains that through the analysis of the essential structures of Dasein's existence we can return to things in the world and discover them as they are originally experienced, as beings within a world, rather than, for example, as distinct and isolable objects. This frequently takes place in our overtly pragmatic dealings with equipmental wholes: 'In understanding itself by way of *things*, the Dasein understands itself as being-in-the-world by way of its world. The shoemaker is not the shoe but, existing, he is his world, a world that first and alone makes it possible to uncover an equipmental contexture as intraworldly and to dwell with it.'[3] However, the world that Dasein encounters in the things that surround it is not only present in this surrounding world of equipment. The world is also always a world filled with others. I see not only myself in intraworldly things, but others too. Heidegger illustrates this by citing a passage from the semi-autobiographical work of the young poet Rainer Maria Rilke, *The Notebooks of Malte Laurids Brigge*, in which we find a detailed description of what is experienced in the broken walls of ruined houses. In this 'broken' equipment the others that are there in the world, but often taken for granted when we are, for example, dwelling in the house with them, become apparent with all their concerns. The walls are crumbling and the houses have stood unoccupied for some time, but the existence of a surrounding-world and a with-world reveals itself to the poet:

> The tenacious life of these rooms refused to let itself be trampled down. It was still there; it clung to the nails that had remained; it stood on the hands breadth remnant of the floor; it had crept together there among the onsets of the corners where there is still a tiny bit of interior space [. . .] There stood the noondays and the illnesses, and the expirings and the smoke of years and the sweat that breaks out under the armpits and makes the clothes heavy, and the stale breath of the mouths and the fusel-oil smell of fermenting feet. There stood the pungency of urine and the burning of soot and the gray reek of potatoes and the strong oily stench of decaying grease . . .[4]

The crucial point for Heidegger is that the poet has not given us a fanciful and wildly imaginative description of these walls. Poetry and creative literature is, he claims, the emergence into words of our existence in the world. The world that is there in these ruined walls is the world as it is for all of us. The fantastic and unusual feat is to show that this is the case and to remind us that we see there all of these others with their whole world of interwoven concerns. This is the world as it originally appears to us, all of us, a world filled with everyday significance that we share with others and that they share with us, even when they are not actually physically present beside us.

In the world we are always with others. Buildings and streets, even when derelict and unused, are still occupied by those who designed them, built them and dwelt in them. Landscapes bear the marks of those who have worked them for hundreds or thousands of years. Even on those rare occasions when we find ourselves somewhere truly untouched by human hand, the others are there, even more hauntingly in their striking absence.[5] Robinson Crusoe on his island, the archetypal solitary figure, is haunted by half of Europe. They are there in the building of his houses, in the baking of his bread, in the umbrella he constructs, in his spiritual exercises and eventually in the way he reacts to and lives along with Friday. It is not primarily in physical proximity that others are there along with us in the world, but in the multifarious ways that we encounter and engage with that world. It is a basic structure of Dasein that we live together as a 'we'. Dasein does not find others in the world and then try to get in touch with them. Its 'being-in-the-world' is already 'being-with' or 'being-with-one-another'.

## ii. THE DICTATORSHIP OF THE ONE

The constitution of this fundamental 'we' is bound to be very different in different cultural and historical circumstances. Our conception of what the 'we', composed of social bonds and political institutions amounts to, is part of the actual ontic situation in which 'we' find ourselves. Heidegger claims that at the ontological level of analysis we are not committed to one particular conception of social life. To claim that 'being-with' is a fundamental structure of Dasein is not, for example, a claim about the natural sociability of human beings. It does not commit one to uphold a claim that human beings are innately peaceful and desirous of social harmony. Conversely, it clearly does not commit us to saying that we are individualistic or that we have a tendency towards social strife. Rather, being basically co-operative and social beings or uncooperative and anti-social beings are both possible ontic actualizations of Dasein's fundamental structure of 'being-with'. To live and conceive of oneself as part of a cohesive social body or as an individual in a society which does not exist apart from the individuals it is composed of are both possible ways in which Dasein can live out its 'being-with'.

Yet it is a fundamental assumption of much modern thought that I start out as an isolated self, that I know myself first and foremost and then I try to get in touch with the world and with others in that world. This assumption reflects Descartes' attempt at the birth of modern philosophy to found our knowledge on something absolutely self-evident and certain. His claim was that he had found this self-evident ground in the shape of the 'I' that thinks. Heidegger, however, argues that it is far from it being self-evident that I am in this individualized way. As he puts it in his 1924 lectures on the *Basic Concepts of Aristotelian Philosophy*:

> The basic assertion that I myself as a living human being in my world, the primary assertion: "I am," is genuinely false. One must say: "I am one." (*ich bin man*) "One" is, "one" undertakes this and that, "one" sees things in such a way. This One is the genuine *how* of everydayness, of average, concrete being-with-one-another.[6]

Descartes' attempt to found thought on the self-evidence of his own being was a turn away from the phenomena. Far from it being the case that I start out alone in my being and thinking, everyone else is implicated in my thoughts and being from the start. Each of us lives with others as a 'self' and yet this self has a peculiar basic structure, a structure which every one of us participates in on an everyday basis. This structure is what Heidegger calls the 'One' and the kind of selfhood that we have in belonging to it 'one's-self'.[7] It is a self in which one is absorbed into others. Belonging to the 'One' Dasein in itself is not being itself. It is as part of this anonymous One that we all generally understand ourselves, our opinions, our expectations, our requirements. Even our own thoughts and attempts to escape from opinion rely upon an understanding of thought, certainty and doubt that is available to 'one'.

The kind of being that we all have as absorbed in one's-self is constituted by constantly reinforced ways of going about things and understanding ourselves. These can differ enormously over time and in different geographical locations. The sheer variety of different standards and mores is well known. Sometimes one quietly fits into the group dynamic and does not stand out. Sometimes one must stand out to be one's-self. Nevertheless, whatever the actual standard by which the One understands itself from day to day, one is in all cases subject to those particular ways of understanding one's-self.

In *Being and Time* Heidegger distinguishes three essential features of the public mode of being of the One: *distantiality, averageness* and *levelling-down*.[8] We are all a part of the crowd, but the crowd can accommodate those who differentiate and distinguish themselves.

In fact, 'one' is frequently concerned with how one is differentiated from others. One is concerned about how others differ, whether such differences should be upheld or levelled out, whether one is falling behind or is ahead of the game.[9] One is with others in taking one's distance. In all one's efforts to distinguish oneself from the crowd or just to be oneself, one is continually measuring oneself against the others and when one puts a *distance* between oneself and others that is only to become further bound to that measure. Averageness means that anything exceptional or unusual is made into something average through the operation of normalization, whereas levelling-down means that one does not even recognize a difference between the average and the unusual. According to Heidegger's analysis of our basic constitution as one's-self, we all serve to uphold certain ways of going about things, standards and measures for getting on and being understood. This is not just some contingent psychological and sociological fact about certain people, but the way in which Dasein is in its world with others. Even those who are said to lack all standards maintain a multitude of them in the most basic ways in which they deal with others, and they are also used by the One as a measure of the standards that are to be maintained. Challenges to prevalent standards are often made in the name of other, perhaps 'higher', standards. Furthermore, their very being as standards requires that they are oblivious to any behavior or mode of existence which is unique or outside of their sphere of recognition. That does not mean that one does not recognize when standards are breached or when someone is not conforming. On the contrary, those who are concerned to uphold standards are notoriously concerned with all breaches and non-conformity. Yet in upholding standards we are inevitably drawn into averageness and levelling-down. One may recognize breaches and non-conformity, but one will do so by judging the existence of others by standards which apply to everyone. Even the most unusual, bizarre or outlandish behavior is categorized as of a certain type and thus positioned on a scale with respect to the 'average'. One may well recognize what is not average, but one cannot recognize what has no place in relation to the average.

We all stand under the orders and live within the order of this anonymous One. Everyone belongs to the One and in doing so could be anyone at all. It is not a particular person or group of people who give the orders. The 'others' that belong to 'one's-self' are not any particular others. Indeed, 'One belongs to the Others oneself and enhances their power.'[10] So each of us is involved in the ordering. Neither is one just the helpless victim of forces of social pressure and control. Rather, one brings these forces to bear upon others and, perhaps above all, upon oneself. In *Being and Time* Heidegger illustrates the phenomenon that he has in mind with examples drawn from modern public life. One makes use of public transport and mass communication methods such as newspapers.[11] Certainly, Heidegger would have no shortage of potential illustrations to add to this list as they were developed and 'made public' during his own lifetime and since his time. Television and the internet are the most obvious. Yet the analysis is not supposed to be solely a diagnosis of the condition of modern mass society, even if certain phenomena in that society build upon and have a particular affinity to the basic existential structure that Heidegger is trying to bring into view.[12] The public realm of the One, however, is in place in one way or another for all Dasein and can just as well be illustrated by fireside stories as by chat rooms or blogs.

Dasein's way of existing in the world is marked by a tendency to take for granted what everyone does and says, what everyone likes and dislikes, and so forth. This tendency is not the preserve of particularly lazy, indolent, uncritical or stupid individuals. Critical discourse and counter-cultural ways of life have their own standards. The consequence of this way of being is that we share a world that is structured and articulated by the patterns of significance that are taken for granted. It is not only how other people appear to us that is dictated by the 'One', but what anything and everything in the world around us signifies and means to us. Worldly significance is articulated and it is articulated first and foremost by everyone. It is through this shared articulation of what is going on around us and what the circumstances are, that we are able to tackle the world.

One lives within the order of the One. One's being is dissolved into the being of the others and the others constitute one's selfhood. Heidegger provocatively calls this the 'real dictatorship of the "One" '.[13] This dictatorship has no figurehead and no center of control or command. One keeps the others in line and they in turn keep one in line. Usually one does not even need to make those standards explicit or to institutionalize them in any formal way. Maintaining order and living up to standards is simply what one does. Order can be imposed, but it can also be inconspicuously diffusing as everyone's expectation. We must not see this as an entirely negative phenomenon; rather, it is utterly ubiquitous and underpins Dasein's life with others anywhere and everywhere. It is the condition for the institution and maintenance of any standards at all, including all of those that one dearly wishes to uphold, such as universal rights. Nevertheless, Heidegger's provocative description reminds us that political regimes of all types can be very well versed in exploiting all the ways in which One maintains order.

Heidegger himself thought he could discern this at work in the 'standardized' social norms of the 1920s' Weimar Republic, but then became notoriously and, for many, unforgivably involved in the devastating dictatorship of National Socialism in the 1930s. That involvement has provoked many important historical and philosophical studies of the relationship between Heidegger's thought and political life. It may be, as some have concluded, that Heidegger's philosophical thought was ultimately lacking in some respect that contributed to his complicity. What cannot be denied is that his thought requires the reader to try to understand how and why such complicity in political disaster and horror took place and still takes place all of the time, rather than to assume complacently that anyone is immune from becoming complicit in such a way. Heidegger's own analysis suggests that the real question is not how one becomes complicit, but how there might be resistance to complicity that is grounded in the ubiquitous way that we are there along with others.

### iii. THE REAL AND THE AUTHENTIC SELF

The kind of being that we all participate in as part of the One may appear to be very insubstantial. Everyone belongs to the One and in so belonging could be anyone at all: 'Everyone is the other, and no one is himself.'[14] If we ask 'who' Dasein is, then the answer can only be that this Dasein is nobody in particular but all of us and each and everyone of us. Yet surprisingly this nobody is far from insubstantial: 'Who is this everyone? It is imperceptible, indefinable, no one – however, it is not nothing but rather the most real reality of our everyday Dasein.'[15] In *Being and Time* Heidegger even uses the scholastic terminology *ens realismum* (the most real being), a term usually used to designate the kind of being which belongs to God, the all-powerful and most substantial being, to describe the

One.[16] In its everyday mode of being with others Dasein finds stability and constancy in its participation in the anonymous self of everyone. The standards that one is subject to need not necessarily be codified into rules and laws. Nor must they be, either literally or metaphorically, commandments set in stone. The reality of the One does not depend upon its being given constitutional or institutional instantiation. On the contrary, the creation of institutions is something made possible on the basis of the everyday social reality that is everyone. The most real reality that belongs to everyone is not in tension with its amorphous and anonymous character, but rather it is because of those characteristics that it forms the constant and substantial way in which Dasein is with others and, as such, in its world. That is because one is provided with a stock of ways to tackle the world and ways of articulating the world, ways of tackling and articulating that we constantly fall back on and rely upon. One's very way of being in the world is clichéd, and because of that it is able to get on in the world.

Is this most substantial and real self our true and authentic self? We have a tendency to assume that the authentic self must be what is most real, substantial and reliable. That self is understood to be constant and always available, even though it may have been accidentally obscured by extraneous and contingent concerns. For Heidegger, this is an inversion of the true situation. For him the 'authentic' or 'proper' self is not the self that we find in the One, nor is it ever available and reliable. It is certainly not something that can be reached by trying to remove ourselves from the world altogether. There could be no such complete removal for a being that is defined as being-in-the-world. Rather, Dasein only finds its authentic self when the substantial and reliable self of the One withdraws. It is not a question of 'getting a hold of yourself' or 'getting a grip on yourself', if that involves separating or differentiating yourself from the world. Rather, the authentic self is distinguished from the self of the One because, 'it has been taken hold of in its own way' in its worldly involvement and its concern for others.[17]

In this distinction of the inauthentic but substantial 'one's-self' and the authentic self, Heidegger is following the great nineteenth century thinkers Søren Kierkegaard and Friedrich Nietzsche. Kierkegaard was particularly influential in the development of some of the key concepts that are used in *Being and Time* to develop the interpretation of the authentic self. Heidegger was always interested in and influenced by Nietzsche, although his most sustained engagement with Nietzsche's thought came later, in the late thirties and early forties. The significance of these two thinkers for Heidegger can be felt most especially in their understanding of the authentic self. Far from being a reliable and constant possession, the authentic or true self is something which needs to be won in some way, as we exist within the crowd or the herd to which we all belong. But it cannot be won by sheer unilateral force of will. Winning my authentic self involves ever renewed and appropriate responses to insights into one's worldly existence that are usually missed because they are articulated in the language that everyone shares.

As with Kierkegaard and Nietzsche too, there is a strong ethical dimension to Heidegger's discussion of the inauthentic self subjected to everyone and its distinction from the authentic self. The authentic self becomes aware that for all the constancy and reliability of the prescriptions and standards that everyone upholds, they have no ultimate grounding in 'the way things must be' that entails that they simply have to be accepted or followed. The authentic self becomes responsible for itself, for its worldly engagement, for its concern for others and finally for the way that it articulates its world. Yet none of this entails that the authentic self is able to fully and finally lift itself clear of the inauthentic self constituted by everyone. There are two reasons why Heidegger resists the claim that his analysis has anything to do with morality, even when it does clearly have ethical import. First, 'moral philosophy' as it is frequently understood is the articulation of general prescriptions and standards and the search for ultimate and inescapable grounds for accepting them. In other words, it is precisely the kind of activity that constitutes the everyday self of the One. The ethical dimension of Heidegger's thought is not about prescribing certain courses of action, but about asking us to distinguish for ourselves between those actions we undertake simply because 'that is what one does' and those that are genuinely our own action. Secondly, as soon as the distinction is made between the inauthentic and the authentic self there is an almost irresistible tendency to think of these selves as belonging to two different sorts of person or two distinct ways of life. It is essential to realize that, so far as Heidegger is concerned, there is no such thing as an authentic life, if that means a life fully and finally extricated from the inauthentic life of the One. It is the life of everyone that forms the *existentiale*, the basic and essential structure of being-with that belongs to every Dasein. Authenticity is *existentiell*, a concrete modification or way of living that is first of all given to us as belonging to everyone: 'Authenticity is only a modification but not total obliteration of inauthenticity.'[18] There is no existence that has finally extricated itself from inauthenticity, only an existence that, finding itself in a world articulated by everyone, renews the effort to make both its individual and collective actions its own.

## iv. LANGUAGE BEARS THE ONE

Heidegger's phenomenological description of the One frequently takes on a negative tone. If it is not possible to finally extricate oneself from this pervasive 'dictatorship', we may understand this as an unfortunate predicament. Such an assessment of the situation as the tragic inevitability of 'falling in' with the crowd or herd might be possible on the basis of the modern thinking of authenticity. Yet there is another side to this coin, one that derives from Heidegger's intensive study of Aristotle in the early 1920s, creating a complex crossing of modern and ancient concepts. The double root of Heidegger's concept of the One means that any straightforward interpretation that tries to see it as an entirely negative phenomenon becomes impossible. The discovery of the *existential* structure of One is in part the outcome of Heidegger's investigation into the roots of universal conceptualization itself, something that makes all philosophical thought possible. Heidegger sought the pre-scientific conditions in the structure of Dasein that allowed the Greeks to develop universal 'scientific' concepts. Our being as part of the anonymous pervasive One is the very condition of the possibility of philosophical and scientific thought.

According to Heidegger's reading, Aristotle gained access to the phenomenon of being-with-one-another as One, which he designated by the Greek term *koinon*, from *koinos*, what is common or shared in common. It was his thinking of this basic structure of Dasein's existence that underpinned Aristotle's understanding of how philosophical and scientific concepts are grounded in our everyday being-in-the-world along with one another. Such concepts are required to have general and universal validity, a demand that can only be made and met on the basis of our being-with as One. If this particular strand of Aristotle's thinking is taken as the foundation of his achievement, as Heidegger thinks it should be, then we can see how philosophy here gains unprecedented access to the condition of its own possibility. As we saw above, in his 1924 lectures on Aristotle, Heidegger claims that the 'I am' of an isolated and individual thinker essentially misinterprets the fundamental situation of Dasein. He goes on to argue that Aristotle's various designations of the basic kind of being that belongs to the human being all point to the same basic phenomenon. Human beings are 'speaking animals' and they are 'political animals'. They are not animals that happen to speak and happen to live together. It is our very being to be 'in common' and as such we speak and live together. We do not speak because we are political nor are we political because we speak. These things are equally fundamental for us and 'co-originary': 'The one is the genuine how of the being of human beings in everydayness, the *genuine bearer of this One is language*. The One maintains itself, has its genuine dominion, in language.'[19]

## v. BETWEEN OUR SELVES

Most of the critical attention given to Heidegger's conception of the self, or rather conceptions of various modes of being a self, focuses on the difference between authentic and inauthentic selfhood. This is only to be expected, since Heidegger locates that difference as the starting point for the continuous attempt to come into possession of our authentic selves. However, this focus might easily lead us to overlook the fact that this distinction is not one that everyone makes. Dasein can exist in such a way that there is no distinction between the authentic and the inauthentic for it. Thus Heidegger also distinguishes between the mode of existence in which authenticity and inauthenticity are differentiated and a mode of existence in which they are undifferentiated:

> We have defined the idea of existence as an ability-to-be, as one which is in each case *mine*, is free either for authenticity or for inauthenticity or for a mode in which neither of these has been differentiated. In starting with average everydayness, our interpretation has heretofore been confined to the analysis of such existing as is either undifferentiated or inauthentic.[20]

Potentially authentic existence is existence between two selves, the inauthentic and the authentic. Authentic existence is a specific existentiell working out and living through of Dasein's existential structure, which is still grounded in the One and remains the same for everyone and anyone. Dasein's ability to be authentic is thus made possible in the specific modification of that existence as One in which Dasein makes a distinction between its authentic and inauthentic self. Authenticity is only possible for those who differentiate between inauthenticity and authenticity. That is why authenticity is not a question of extricating oneself from the One once and for all. Rather it is a question of whether one distinguishes between the self that belongs to the One and the self that takes its own way of living out the possibilities made available to it as genuinely its own. If Dasein can maintain that difference, then it makes authenticity and inauthenticity into possibilities for itself.

A life in which authenticity is a possibility is not a life of flawless adherence to a self that is utterly self-made. There is no such self, there is only the self that is made and articulated in common. Authenticity is the attempt to make a self in common that is also a self that I make my own. Neither is an inauthentic existence, understood as such, an utterly abject life that contains no glimmer of emancipation from the rule of the One. On the contrary, when it makes a difference to us whether we are able to claim ourselves as our own, then we may be inauthentic but authenticity is a possibility. There is no existence that takes complete ownership of itself or completely disclaims itself. Rather, there is a mode of existence that maintains a difference for itself between the two, but there is also an existence for which it makes no difference at all.

# CHAPTER 5

# FINDING ONESELF IN A MOOD

The heart is the key to the world and to life.

*Templitz Fragments*, 36

We saw in the last chapter that Heidegger's thought of becoming an authentic self does not involve extricating 'oneself' once and for all from everyday being-in-the-world with others. It involves a modification or transformation of the way in which we inhabit the world together. In order to see how such a modification can take place we need to take a closer look at exactly how it is that Dasein is in the world.

If we begin to think about how it is that we are in our world all of the time, then one thing about Dasein's worldy relations is striking. Whatever it is that we are doing in the world, whether we are immersed in what we are doing, lost in drifting about from one thing to another, thinking intently about some problem or distantly appraising something, we are always feeling one way or another about ourselves and the world we are in. Dasein does not occasionally have emotions, but its emotions are an essential condition of its being. They may sometimes be very intense, so that other feelings seem like nothing in comparison. They may sometimes come and go fleetingly, giving the impression that they are simply added on as optional extras to our engagements with the world. Yet Heidegger argues that emotions and moods cannot be properly understood as optional extras to our engagement with the world. Nor can they be understood as 'primitive' ways of engaging that can be overcome and mastered by ways that are without feeling altogether. Moods come in many different forms, but they are a fundamental part of every way that Dasein is in the world.

## i. WHERE DO MOODS BELONG?

When we try to think about the feelings we have and the moods that we are in a certain difficulty quickly becomes apparent. On the one hand, moods are something that happen to us. They come over us and they can feel overwhelming, not even part of us, something which *affects* us but that is not our own. Not only do we sometimes refuse to take responsibility for our moods, but we recognize that moods can affect the responsibility which we expect ourselves and others to take for our thoughts and actions. Legal systems may recognize that people can be overwhelmed by fear or rage and that as a result they are maybe less responsible for themselves because they are less themselves. So moods seem to take us away from ourselves. On the other hand, we think of moods as making us truly ourselves. We speak of our 'true feelings' about something or someone, not only as though we are willing to recognize those feelings as belonging to us among other things, but as though they were the very heart of who we are.

Do our moods belong to us or do we belong to our moods? If 'belonging to us' is taken to mean that our moods are entirely under the control of a faculty that itself remains entirely unaffected by mood then moods do not belong to us, because there is no such isolated faculty. One can certainly learn to affect one's mood as everybody does to one extent or another. One gets to know situations and circumstances that tend to produce certain affective responses and one can manipulate one's circumstances to a certain extent. We may learn techniques that tend to put us into a certain mood. But none of this puts us in absolute control over our mood, such that we can simply decide to feel this way or that. I may not feel towards these circumstances today as I have done in the past. In any case, I am not in complete control of my circumstances. I can manipulate them to a certain degree, but I am always thrown into a situation which affords me certain specific possibilities.

There is no position devoid of feeling from which one could control and manipulate one's feelings like a supervisor in a control room. Rather, as Heidegger argues, 'when we master a mood, we do so by way of a counter-mood; we are never free of moods.'[1] The creation of moods takes place in many different ways and for many different reasons. Dealing with moods is not one thing we do amongst others, but something we are engaged in all the time. For example, Heidegger points us towards Aristotle's investigation of rhetoric, not as an inquiry into decorative turns of phrase or manipulative crowd pleasing, but as an attempt to, 'understand the possibilities of moods in order to arouse them and guide them aright.'[2]

We are not totally at the mercy of particular moods but neither are moods always at our beck and call. All moods have this double structure of gripping me and in so gripping me revealing myself and my way of engaging and being open to the world, such that I may get to grips with my being in that world in one way or another. Heidegger creates a new term to designate this *existentiale* of being-in-the-world by way of being in a mood. In German the question 'How are you feeling?' (*Wie befinden Sie sich?*) roughly means 'How are you doing?' but more literally means, 'How do you find yourself?' From this notion of finding oneself disposed towards one's situation in a certain manner Heidegger creates the term *Befindlichkeit*, 'disposition', in which one finds oneself already disposed towards things in a certain way.[3] In English we now sometimes ask 'How are you doing?' which expresses feeling as this sense of having been and still being disposed towards things in a certain way. The point of this shift in terminology is to try to get us out of the habit of thinking about feelings and emotions as primarily belonging to an isolated subject, as being 'all in the head'. Feelings and emotions belong to us as beings that are always out in the world, disposed to that world in a certain way. There are two kinds of answer to the question of how one finds oneself or how one is 'getting on'. One might reply, 'I'm elated' or 'miserable' or 'sad'. On the other hand, it is equally possible to reply, 'I'm trying to finish my essay' or 'I'm going on holiday next week' or 'I'm meeting James for lunch'. Each kind of answer invites elucidation in terms of the other. So following the first kind of reply I might ask: 'Why are you elated? What is going on to make you so happy?', while in reply to the second kind of response I may go on to inquire, 'How are you feeling about going to lunch with James? Are you excited or apprehensive?' The circumstances and the feeling are not originally separated, but are two sides of the same phenomenon. The phenomenon of Dasein's disposition is not originally subjective or objective, 'all in the head' or 'out there independently of my being there'. The disposition is Dasein's way of opening itself to its circumstances and its openness towards its circumstances reciprocally disposes it in a certain way.

Understanding is not something which comes after Dasein's being disposed towards its situation in a certain way. Nor does it only develop a disposition after it has previously come to a certain understanding of its circumstances. Disposition and understanding are both equally basic ways, or as Heidegger puts it 'co-originary' *existentiales*, in which Dasein is in its world. Disposition and understanding always come together with the articulation of a world in common. In being disposed Dasein is in a mood. The etymology of the English term suggests that mood used to be understood as integrated with our understanding of the world and ourselves. In Old English, to be 'mōdig' was to be brave, proud and high-spirited. To be 'mōdful' was to be proud as a disposition towards the world and oneself (In modern German the related term 'Mut' means courage). 'Mōdcræft', however, was intelligence and 'mōdgeðanc' was thought, understanding or mind, suggesting a fundamental link between being in a mood and thought of any kind that is commonly denied or misunderstood. 'Emotional intelligence' is not just one special kind of intelligence, i.e., intelligence concerning emotions. Emotions are the conditions for varying kinds of intelligence. When we say that a certain kind of thinking is 'cold', 'determined', even 'ruthless' that is not an indication that it is without emotion, but quite the contrary, that it requires a very particular kind of emotion. So Heidegger argues that: 'A disposition always has its understanding, even if it merely keeps it suppressed. Understanding always has its mood.'[4] Finding oneself disposed towards one's circumstances is an existential structure of Dasein. Our circumstances affect our mood and our mood in turn opens an understanding of circumstances. There is a kind of unavoidable reciprocity within mood that accounts for the impression that moods belong to us and do not belong to us at the same time. Through my mood circumstances reveal themselves and as they reveal themselves they affect my mood. This does not take place as one thing after another, but as a continual reciprocity of mood and circumstance.

## ii. THE FUNDAMENTAL TONE OF ATTUNEMENT

To understand the central role that Heidegger assigns to moods in every aspect of Dasein's existence, including the possibility of philosophical thought, we must turn towards a distinction that he makes between different levels of disposition. We can then go on to look at a number of moods that bring about philosophical thought itself. The distinction in question is that between moods in which one is disposed towards circumstances within the world and 'fundamental moods' in which one is disposed towards the world as such.

We can begin by returning to the history of the English word 'mood'. That history records a much later meaning than that of the spirited intellect, with a quite different etymological lineage, a second sense that nevertheless came to significantly affect the first. This second sense of mood derived from a modification of 'mode', came to mean the grammatical function of a verb or the kind of musical scale. This sense of the English 'mood' accords with a second term employed by Heidegger in his thinking of disposition. *Stimmung*, 'mood' or 'attunement',[5] originally meant the tuning of a musical instrument, but now means disposition or emotion. However, *Stimmung* also means the atmosphere of a place or an event. A dark and misty forest might have an eerie atmosphere, while a musical concert might have a fun and lively atmosphere. It is not the case that Dasein simply projects moods on to the world around it. It already finds the world attuned in a certain way and it can attune itself to that mood or remain out of tune with it. Moods occur as Dasein attunes itself to the places that it inhabits and the events that it participates in. However, there are also moods that attune us not to particular circumstances, but to our sheer being attuned and being open to a world at all.

Heidegger argues that in its everyday moods Dasein is disposed and attuned towards things and circumstances within the world. In our concern for the things in our surrounding world we are disposed in this way or that towards the involved referential whole of the equipment that we deal with and we are disposed towards others in being-with them. In *Being and Time* the analysis concentrates on fear.[6] Fear is always fear of something. I can be afraid of a wild animal or a hurricane or another person insofar as they are strong, violent, overpowering and dangerous. I can be afraid of a coming exam, of losing my job or being left alone in the dark. I am afraid of this or that because it has the power to break in upon and disrupt my concerned dealings with things in the world. If I was not involved with things in the world in this way, then there would be nothing to be afraid of. Fear also has a temporal direction that comes along with it. I am afraid of what is coming up or coming upon me.[7] Other everyday dispositions or moods will display similar features. I may be pleased because I have found the hammer that I lost, which will allow me to complete the shed I am building. I may be happily anticipating my friend's birthday party next week. In each case I am disposed in this way because of my concerned involvement in my circumstances and caring-for others.

Diverse as these dispositions towards things in the world are, their analysis is not the end of the story. Dasein can also be attuned in such a way that it is not disposed towards particular things or circumstances. There are moods that are not brought about by concerned anticipation of this or that encounter or occurrence. Rather, these are moods in which we open up the whole involved context of equipmental reference that we inhabit as our world. In such moods we are not disposed towards this or that possibility, but rather towards the whole referential system of meanings, the 'worldhood of the world', in which any such possibilities make sense to us in such a way that we can be well or ill disposed towards them. The moods in which Dasein is disposed not towards something within the world, but towards the world itself as a meaningful whole, are what Heidegger calls 'fundamental moods' or 'fundamental attunements'.

Nevertheless, even if we make such a distinction, there is still clearly some kind of connection between everyday moods directed towards circumstances within the world and fundamental moods directed towards the world as such. The connection is not a straightforward derivation of one from the other, such that my disposition towards this or that upcoming occurrence would follow on in a determinate fashion from my having previously been disposed towards the world itself in a particular way. Rather, a fundamental attunement is in some ways comparable to the 'fundamental tone' in a complex sound. The fundamental tone is the basis for any overtone which sounds together with it. Similarly, Heidegger argues that a fundamental mood or attunement, disposing us towards the world as such, is the basis upon which we have dispositions towards our circumstances within the world.

Ludwig Wittgenstein was clearly attuned to what Heidegger calls fundamental moods. In the *Tractatus Logico-Philosophicus*, published in 1921 six years before *Being and Time*, Wittgenstein claims that our fundamental relation to the world can change the world, not by changing the involved connections of things within the world, i.e., by manipulating what is brought to light in the world, but by changing the 'limits of the world', that is, the whole context of involvements. We do not transform the things that can be expressed in language, but the whole articulation of the world in which such expression takes place. Wittgenstein remarks:

> In brief, the world must thereby become quite another. It must so to speak wax and wane as a whole.
>
> The world of the happy is quite another from that of the unhappy.[8]

A mood that sets the tone for our whole articulation of the world in this way is not the kind of mood brought on by understanding certain circumstances. Nevertheless, it is what makes us open and susceptible to joyous appreciation of what is coming up on the one hand, or fearful in miserable trepidation on the other. The whole world of the happy is quite another from that of the unhappy and that in turn is the basis for each to be affected by the circumstances that they encounter within that world.

### iii. NOTHING TO BE ANXIOUS ABOUT

The fundamental mood that Heidegger attempts to attune us to in *Being and Time* is anxiety. He notes that fear and anxiety have very rarely been distinguished and this is because they are clearly kindred phenomena.[9] Nevertheless they are distinct, being related to one another as fundamental mood and everyday concerned disposition. As we have just seen, the distinction turns around that which Dasein is disposed towards in each case. In the case of fear one is disposed towards some occurrence in the world that is coming up or coming upon one. So what am I disposed towards in anxiety? Strangely enough, it is nothing at all. It is not a thing or occurrence that shows up within the world that makes me anxious. The source of my anxiety has no particular location, I cannot see it coming upon me from here or there. I am anxious in the face of nothing and my anxiety comes out of nowhere. This 'nothing' and 'nowhere' allow not particular circumstances and things to become apparent, but the whole world in which circumstances and things appear.

What I am anxious in the face of is actually my whole world: 'That in the face of which one has anxiety is being-in-the-world as such.'[10]

Since it is the kind of being that Dasein is to be in the world, to be anxious in the face of being-in-the-world as such is at one and the same time to be anxious in the face of itself. It is not anxiety about any particular aspect of its life or personal characteristics. Such things are only significant within a world. For example, I might have a social anxiety to do with the clothes I am wearing or the way that I speak. That anxiety might not manifest itself as a completely determinate fear, such as the ridiculing laughter that I anticipate from someone. It might still be relatively amorphous, although I will have a certain sense of where the 'danger' is coming from. Alternatively my social anxiety might be solidified into a vast array of particular and determinate fears. In any case, whether such an anxiety is particularized to a greater or lesser extent, it is not what Heidegger understands by the fundamental mood of anxiety. If I am fearful about this or that, even if my anxiety is relatively form-less; I can be anxious in that way only because that which I am anxious about has significance within an involved world that is already articulated along with others. In fundamental anxiety, how-ever, I am anxious in the face of that world of significations itself as a whole.

In anxiety we experience the world and thus ourselves in a way that we do not in our everyday concerned dealings. There are two sides to this experience. On the one hand, the significance of the world withdraws. This happens when it becomes apparent that the whole involved world of significations, which it is my being as Dasein to inhabit, is not something that can be securely possessed because it is not a thing at all. The world can no longer be taken for granted as the more or less reliable ground for all my concern. The world is the whole of what is intelligible and is the whole spectrum of Dasein's possibilities. In anxiety Dasein feels that it is 'uncanny', or 'not-at-home'.[11] On an everyday basis the world is experienced as familiar, reliable and trustworthy. That does not mean that every-thing in that world is reliable; on the contrary, involvements break-down all of the time, as we have seen. Yet these breakdowns are themselves familiar to us, so that even if one of such and such a kind has not occurred before we can go about repairing it. Neither does the experience of the uncanny necessarily come when we are put into a situation that we are not well acquainted with, for example, when we are among people whose language and customs we do not understand. It may be that we simply get on with learning that language and those customs. We will experience many things that we cannot make sense of, but we need not experience the way in which we are in a world within which things make sense or fail to make sense to us. The experience of the uncanny, on the other hand, does not necessarily come along with breakdowns in intelligibility. The uncanny is experienced when the involved whole within which Dasein finds things intelligible or unintelligible withdraws. This can come when there is a breakdown of involvement or when Dasein finds itself in very unusual and unknown circumstances, but it is equally possible that the experience comes when everything is running well and when it is in the most familiar of settings. The world as the whole of that which is significantly involved, 'ready-to-hand' and ready to be tackled, is experienced as insignificant.[12] Even when things become overt in the midst of their involvement, when they are inconvenient or lost or broken, it is generally their significance which becomes overt, not the whole world that first lends them their significance. When Dasein is caught up in the world it is in the midst of this continuous conversion of things from the smooth running reference to one another into overt recalcitrance and back again. In anxiety this whole is not itself inconvenient or broken or lost, but it withdraws from Dasein as a whole.

The other side of this experience is that Dasein experiences itself as *individualized*. As the world withdraws Dasein no longer experiences itself as a number of significant possibilities which just happen to present themselves, as it does when it is caught up in the world trying to choose between the various options. In anxiety Dasein experiences possibilities not simply as set in place for it by the world, but the world of possibility as itself something to be chosen. Dasein is enabled to *freely choose its possibilities*.[13] The involved equipment within the world, pressing in its significance in everyday life, is no longer pressing. But we experience this release itself as oppressive, because it means that we cannot now rely upon the everyday familiarity of one's-self to choose for us. Nevertheless, in order to be chosen, possibilities must be articulable within the world that we share with everyone. Freedom does not mean that I can design and manipulate my world as a whole from scratch. Rather, the freedom to choose my possibilities, which for Heidegger is the most original sense of freedom, is freedom to choose the whole of significance into which I am thrown as *my own*. Freedom understood as selection from ready-made options or as the creation of a range of options is something that only makes sense within the world of involved significance. In individualization I do not leave the world altogether or become one thing among others in the world. I am in the world that we articulate together as One, but I no longer choose simply on the basis that this is what 'one does'. This leaves me to become the basis of my own decisions. Thus fundamental attunement is necessary for becoming more freely open to the world of possibilities that we are always open to in one way or another.

### iv. THE DEPTHS OF BOREDOM AND LOVE

Is anxiety the only fundamental mood or attunement in which I am individualized in the face of the world as such? In 'What is Metaphysics?' the inaugural lecture that Heidegger delivered when he was made full professor at Freiburg in 1929, he claims both that anxiety has its own unique characteristics and that there are other fundamental moods that can be awoken in us. Anxiety makes manifest the 'nothing'.[14] That is, it comes out of nowhere and when it has passed we feel that it amounts to nothing, but in experiencing it we experience the fact that the ground of our own existence, the world of involved significance, is itself groundless. In being 'held out' into this nothing we not only choose but freely choose our own possibilities. There are, nevertheless, other fundamental moods. Most prominently Heidegger describes what he calls 'profound boredom'.[15] In such boredom it is not this or that particular thing that bores me. I am not bored by this book or that film. Everything bores me and thus everything becomes indifferent to me. It might as well be this book or film as any other. In profound boredom the 'whole' becomes manifest in my indifference towards everything.

Heidegger takes up the mood of profound boredom and subjects it to a sustained analysis in a lecture course of the same year. A full semester of the lectures published as *The Fundamental Concepts of Metaphysics: World, Finitude, Solitude* is devoted to boredom. There Heidegger actually distinguishes three forms of boredom. The first form occurs when we are bored with something in a particular situation.[16] I try to kill time by distracting myself. If I am bored with this book I try another one, or I try going for a walk or watching television or something else. In the second form of boredom, I become bored with something upon the occasion of a particular situation, but what I become bored with is not a particular thing or situation, but I become bored with killing time itself.[17] I am bored with all the things that I use to distract myself and bored with passing the time. So I end up not only bored with this particular book and with my whole situation, but with all my efforts to change it so as to keep myself occupied. Finally, in the third form of boredom I am no longer bored with this particular book or the whole situation in which I try to distract myself, but experience that 'It is boring for one'.[18] No longer is it any particular thing or situation that bores me. The 'it' which is boring is nothing in particular. It is not even me in particular who is bored. One is bored and indifferent to the whole world.

So it turns out that boredom can lead to the uncanny sense of the nothing, but in such a way that one is constantly trying to fill this nothing while being left empty in boredom. If, however, one does not try to fill the boredom, but experiences it as such, then it can lead us towards the world itself and thus individualization. In profound boredom I am bored with myself, not with any features of my own particular existence, but with existence as such. Not only that, but boredom has a temporal character which becomes more and more overt as one's boredom becomes deeper. In boredom time stretches itself out. Heidegger makes much of the fact that the German term for 'boredom' is *Langeweile*, literally, a 'long while'.[19] Heidegger is particularly interested in boredom as a fundamental mood because of this unavoidably temporal character that points towards the temporalization that ultimately is Dasein's existence. However, boredom does not in the first instance individualize us in our own temporalization, but disperses us into the One. It is boring for one. In boredom we are entranced by the world as it belongs to everyone. But that does not mean that in profound boredom there is no hope of individualization. Heidegger argues that in the profound experience of this dispersal into a world that is completely indifferent, in the depths of boredom I am liable to be awakened any moment by the shock of my own entrancement. In being entranced by the expanse of time I am also impelled to an extremity which ruptures that entracement.[20] We might say, I am made anxious by the depths of boredom.

Perhaps surprisingly, one further fundamental mood that Heidegger mentions in his 1929 inaugural lecture is love:

Another possibility of such manifestation [of beings as a whole] is concealed in our joy in the presence of the Dasein – and not simply of the person – of a human being whom we love.[21]

Why is Heidegger careful to say that it is not simply joy at the presence of a person whom we love that would allow for the manifestation of beings as a whole? The point is that love is a fundamental mood only when it opens us to the whole world of the one whom we love. I can be pleased by someone's characteristics, such as his or her physical characteristics or personal characteristics. All of this is nevertheless a disposition towards someone that is encountered within the world. In the depths of love I am not only pleased by personal characteristics, however unusual and unique, but I feel joy at the whole world that another Dasein opens up. I see not only all those things that are significant to them and feel those things to be significant to me also, but I also see the whole world within which things can be significant to them. I open along with them to possibilities and things of potential significance which have not yet come into view. We share a world and the possibilities that are open to us together. Insofar as we are absorbed in that world and in one another then love does not make the world manifest and does not individualize us. However, the implication seems to be that in experiencing the fundamental attunement that makes such absorption possible, it might *individualize us together* as we freely choose our possibilities.

Heidegger does not pursue this hint about love. He does not subject it to the interrogation and depth of analysis to which he subjects anxiety and boredom. Does this mean that he has a propensity towards gloomy 'negative' moods and a suspicious tendency to valorize them as leading the way to deep insights? He certainly denies that this is the case, claiming in 'What is Metaphysics?' that: 'The anxiety of those who are daring cannot be opposed to joy or even to the comfortable enjoyment of tranquilized bustle. It stands – outside of all opposition – in cheerful alliance with the cheerfulness and gentleness of creative longing.'[22] He requires us to reassess what is 'positive' and 'negative' in our dispositions and moods. This is not the suggestion that we need to experience a variety of feelings, including negative and gloomy moods, in order to appreciate more uplifting moods as well. It does not mean that we need to have negative emotions in order to appreciate positive ones. All of that may be true. But Heidegger's reassessment of moods invites us to see that more fundamental than the difference between positivity in the sense of being pleased with things and negativity in the sense of being displeased by them is the difference between that experience of our moods that makes us 'positively' aware of particular things and circumstances and experiences of the depth of mood, the 'negativity' of which removes us into an encounter with the world of our possibilities as such.

If there are a number of fundamental moods and in fact any disposition at all is grounded in a fundamental mood, then why choose any one to pursue over another? There is no ultimate reason that can be given as to where one should start in a philosophical questioning that requires us to become attuned to ourselves and the world in one way or another. Where to begin is ultimately a question of which mood one finds oneself attuned to and gripped by. Nevertheless, Heidegger does move towards the view that there are some fundamental moods to which we are particularly susceptible in particular historical times. He felt boredom as pervasive of his times.[23] This does not mean, however, that Heidegger saw everyone as constantly displaying signs of boredom. We generally flee from fundamental moods, so one sign of the pervasiveness of profound boredom might well be that everyone takes an excessive interest in everything they come across. Heidegger shares this important insight with Kierkegaard, to whom he refers in a footnote to the analysis of anxiety in *Being and Time* and at greater length in *The Fundamental Concepts of Metaphysics*.[24] As Kierkegaard saw, one does not have to constantly feel anxious to exist in a way determined by anxiety nor does one have to feel miserable to be in the depths of despair.[25] One does not need to constantly *feel* bored in order to *be* bored. Similarly, I may be in love and unaware of it, unable to recognize the way in which it illuminates every circumstance I find myself in.

What then, if we are assailed by various dispositions, but do not know where to start because we have never felt anything like these 'fundamental attunements'? What if we have never been anxious in the face of being-in-the-world as such, or profoundly bored or in love to such a degree? Heidegger's response is that even if we have not felt them as such nor become awakened or attuned to them, fundamental moods pervade our existence. They cannot disappear altogether, since they are the condition of the possibility of the everyday dispositions that open me to my circumstances in the world. Fundamental moods do not disappear in everyday dispositions, but the experience of them requires that we awaken them by attending to them rather than constantly trying to cover them over with our latest worry, interest or infatuation. The problem is not one of trying to work out which mood one is really gripped by, but of allowing oneself to be gripped at all: 'Thus we shall not speak of "ascertaining" a fundamental attunement in our philosophizing, but of *awakening* it.'[26]

# CHAPTER 6

# MEANING AND TRUTH

Man has his being in truth – if he sacrifices truth he sacrifices himself. It is not a question of lying – but of acting against one's convictions.

*Miscellaneous Observations*, 38

There is one assumption that has guided a great deal of inquiry into meaning and truth and their relation, shared by many ancient and modern thinkers. That assumption is that there are certain 'linguistic items' that can be the bearers of meaning and truth. For example, a series of sounds produced by the vocal chords or a string of marks made on paper may not be meaningful in themselves, but they are thought of as potential bearers of meaning, perhaps because some isolable act or cognition lends them meaning. Following upon the identification of linguistic items as such potential meaning and truth bearers, there are a number of important questions that can be posed. What is it for a particular linguistic item to be meaningful and/or true? How do we identify a linguistic item as meaningful or true? Are there particular conditions which have to be fulfilled in order for a particular linguistic item to be a potential meaning or truth bearer? What is the minimum 'unit' of meaning? What structure must a string of sounds or marks have if it is to be a potential bearer of meaning? How might we move from understanding the meaning of a linguistic item to determining its truth value?

As we have seen, Heidegger thought that the meaningfulness of any 'item' depends upon its being not first and foremost an item at all, but rather caught up and involved in the whole of worldly significance. So much so that certain distinctive kinds of occurrence have to take place in order for us to be able to identify and isolate individual 'items' in the first place. Everything refers us onwards to something else. Signs are first and foremost special kinds of equipment that do not point towards isolated items, but make explicit the involved context of the world to the Dasein that is concerned with it.[1] In fact, anything whose being is of a different kind to Dasein can be significant only within Dasein's world. At the same time, any particular thing or circumstance that lacks significance and is, for example, meaningless or absurd, is so within that world. Things or events that are devoid of meaning can break in upon and move against the meaningfulness of Dasein's world as a whole, moving to destroy that world by destroying Dasein.[2] But the very possibility of anything being understood as 'senseless', depends upon a Dasein for whom there is a world.

This is not to say that none of the questions that are raised within the ambit of projects that try to locate meaning and truth bearers are legitimate. They have their own legitimacy and can produce significant results regarding, for example, the conditions under which a string of sounds or marks is likely to be regarded as meaningful or not. Here the ideal of knowledge that we possess for the study is that of natural science, which Heidegger argues, is 'the legitimate task of grasping the present-at-hand [i.e., items within the world] in its essential unintelligibility.'[3] Language can be made into an object of study in this way, but then we miss the referential whole, the meaningful event of Dasein's being-in-the-world, that is the ultimate condition for anything being meaningful or for its lacking meaning.

It is therefore not the case that an item of any kind can bear meaning in and of itself. Rather, the significant whole that is Dasein's world bears items within it, some of which can be used as signs to point out and make explicit what is required in our involvement. The attempt to isolate the bearers of meaning as items or complexes of items that are meaningful insofar as they refer to other items or complexes of items is a false start. If we think of language as that which allows for things within the world to be meaningful, that which articulates the world in one way or another, then language does not have a location within the world. Language is not 'in my head' any more than it is 'there on the pages of this book'. Language is a facet of the way in which Dasein is in its world and as such its 'location' is in Dasein's condition of being in its world.[4]

Language is what takes place, for example, when I read a book, or speak with someone, or 'read' their hand gestures, or understand what is going on in one situation or another.

When meaning is understood as the reference of one thing to another, whether or not they be physical things like marks and sounds, or 'special' mental things like thoughts, then truth can be understood as a special kind of reference in which two items or complexes of items match up in a particular way that one is 'adequate' to the other. On the other hand, if meaningfulness is ultimately not located in any particular items, but is the character of Dasein's being in its world, then our approach to both meaning and truth will need to be radically transformed.

## i. LAYING OUT UNDERSTANDING

Along with articulating the world in a certain way and being disposed towards it, Dasein understands it. That does not mean that Dasein ever has the whole world laid out to view as a complete collection of items together with their abstract relations. But it can and always does understand the world, in the sense of *being able* to follow through certain possibilities that the equipmental whole that it is thrown into affords it, to articulate that whole by speaking with others and to feel disposed towards its circumstances within that whole.

Importantly, failure to understand is implicated in our ability to understand. Nobody is ever completely competent in their tackling of the world. While I may have mastered a whole range of practices, such that I do not need to plan out what I am doing in advance or be consciously aware of what I am doing, there will always be more to learn about how to go about in the world. Even as I set about things in ways that I am very familiar with, something may always come up, showing that I do not have complete mastery. In a world where understanding never failed, nothing would ever show up at all, because everything would be seamlessly referred onwards. Since so-called 'linguistic' abilities are abilities that we have as beings that understand the world, the same is true in their case. I may be a fully competent speaker of a language, which will mean that on the whole I need pay no attention to my ability. Yet I cannot be the complete master of a language, including my 'native tongue', any more than I can ever completely master my world. While nobody is ever completely competent in their ability to make their way in the world and thus to understand that world, nobody is ever utterly incompetent either. Dasein may lack certain abilities altogether. It may be relatively helpless and lack the ability to fend for itself. We are all in this condition for large parts of our lives. But insofar as it is in the world at all, that is, insofar as it exists, Dasein always has some ability to get along with the things around it and others who are there with it. That ability may be very underdeveloped, it may generally be unconscious and inexplicit, but it is still an ability to be: 'In every understanding of the world, existence is understood with it, and *vice versa.*'[5]

We always begin with some kind of understanding of the world and how to go about things, even if it is not well worked out. Within this understanding of the world we can be presented with things or with behavior that we do not understand. We may not know what to make of it at all. We may feel that in this instance we are 'clueless'. However, there will always be some clues or possibilities that we can follow up. The clues that we follow may not lead to a correct understanding, at least initially, but it is only by following them that we can possibly come to any further understanding.

For example, in an archaeological dig I may unearth a shard of glass. I had no idea until this moment that the people of the era in question used glass at all. Everything else I know about them tells against it. And yet here it is and it looks like it definitely belonged to their 'equipment'. At first I think that it might be a broken vessel, because I know that neighboring people at the time did use such vessels and there may have been trade relations between the two. I come to an understanding of this shard through having some prior understanding of what may have been possible for these people. In the end it turns out that this shard was not part of a vessel at all, that they used no such vessels. Instead it was a tiny shard that was fitted into an arrowhead. I come to this understanding also through fitting the glass more adequately into my understanding of their world. And in doing so I also get a more adequate understanding of that world, which will allow me to better understand other findings, and so on. Understanding, therefore, has what Heidegger calls a 'fore-structure'.[6] That is to say, I always have some understanding to begin with and that *opens the way* to better understanding.

Furthermore, understanding and interpretation are inseparable. Usually we think that interpretation is required if we do not understand something and that after a process of interpretation we come to understand. However, because we always have some understanding of how to get on which opens the way to further understanding, we do not move from no understanding to full understanding, but from relatively little understanding to better understanding. Furthermore, we have seen that 'interpretation' of its own existence is the kind of being that belongs to Dasein as such, so those instances that we call acts of interpretation, for example, interpreting a literary text or the speaker of a foreign language, are only specific and exaggerated instances of this continuous interpretation. Interpretation is the 'laying out' of the place of things in the world as we understand it.[7] When equipment comes explicitly to view in some kind of breakdown or disruption, Dasein can perform a certain kind of interpretation by 'taking things apart', with a view to putting them back together in better working order. However, what takes place here is not interpretation as such, but only a peculiar instance of it. Dasein already lays things out without the necessity of taking them apart. What is involved is bringing into view the specific referential relatedness of the involved whole and the possibilities that it affords us. I lay out these referential possibilities. That means that I see that which I am interpreting 'as' this, that or the other. I may come to see the berries on this bush *as* food, or *as* a dye for clothes or *as* medicine. These are not exclusive or exhaustive interpretations; the berries can appear as all this and more. What I do not see first of all is the bare berries and then 'read into them' these possibilities. In interpretation I do not create the 'as' that allows me to see the berries 'as food' or 'as dye'. The 'as' was already there in each possible understanding, even when I did not have it in view. For Heidegger, interpretation is the laying out of the 'as-structure': 'In dealing with what is environmentally ready-to-hand by interpreting it circumspectively, we "see" it *as* a table, a door, a carriage or a bridge; but what we have thus interpreted need not necessarily be taken apart by making an assertion that definitely characterizes it.'[8] Understanding is the understanding of the possible roles that things can play within the world. In interpretation Dasein brings some of those possibilities into view and can thus come to further its understanding of its own possibilities as it goes about its world. Understanding is not the result of interpretation but interpretation is the development of understanding: 'In interpretation, understanding does not become something different. It becomes itself.'[9]

Dasein's ability to be in its world gives to the tackle involved in those abilities its whole range of possible significance. Interpretative understanding is not restricted to certain kinds of item, such as vocal sounds or marks on paper, but takes place in Dasein's concernful dealings with its world. This is nicely illustrated by R. G. Collingwood, a philosopher, historian and archaeologist, who knew all about the difficulties we face in interpreting individual items, single occurrences or isolated actions that have been severed from their worldly involvement. Collingwood realized that if we are able to return those items, occurrences or actions to the involved whole to which they belong, then we can understand them and continue to interpret their significance. Thinking of those who claim that we cannot understand the actions of Caesar because he is not around for us to ask him what he meant by his action, Collingwood remarks: 'These are the people who, if they met you one Saturday afternoon with a fishing-rod, creel, and camp-stool, walking towards the river, would ask: "Going fishing?" '[10] In this scenario he has not said anything, but it should be easy to understand that he is going fishing. Similarly we can understand and continue to interpret Caesar's actions not because we have any particular document or piece of physical evidence before us, but because we can enter into the world in which those documents and physical items had meaning and in doing so we give them meaning once more. Now when Collingwood thinks of this encounter on the way to the river, interpretative understanding of the 'as-structure' that belongs to the tackle he is carrying and the direction he is walking in makes it open to view that he is going fishing. What is amusing here is that the question seems to ask for confirmation of that. However, it is quite possible that in asking this question we are not asking for such confirmation, but asking for a further clarification of what is going on. For example, we might be surprised that he is going fishing because he usually gets his fish from the market. We are asking for a further clarification of how his circumstances have changed and thus a further clarification and interpretation of the world of involvements in which he is engaged. Further clarification of precisely how it is that things are involved for someone as they go about the world is always possible, so long as we see that this is what is involved in interpretation, rather than fixing 'the meaning' of any particular item. However, there may come a point when even the person so engaged is unable to provide further clarification. Interpretation must come to an end somewhere, but that is only because we are finite beings who can no more have a final and complete understanding of the possibilities of the world we open up and are engaged with, than we can be in the world without any understanding of it at all.

## ii. DISCLOSING AND ENCLOSING AN HORIZON

Understanding thus takes place within the field of potential significance that Dasein is open to as its way of being-in-the-world. The question of truth then becomes, for Heidegger, a question concerning the essentially finite way in which Dasein opens up such a world. For him, truth is not primarily a question of finding some linguistic items that are the bearers of meaning and then trying to discover how and why it is that some are understood to be correct, while others are false. This is one way of going about things, but one that relies upon there being a field of meaning, a 'world', opened up for us in the first place. It is inquiry into how worldly significance is opened up by and for Dasein that is the fundamental question of truth, while inquiry into the truth and falsity of statements and assertions is something which can take place within a world. The opening up of a world is truth in the primary sense.

In *Being and Time* Heidegger formally indicates the characteristics of the opening up of the world as the field of possible meaning or significance in two ways. He characterizes it as the *disclosure* of the world.[11] At the same time he characterizes it as a *projection* of the world.[12] In their immediate connotations these two indications point us towards an element of passivity in the case of disclosure and of activity in the case of projection. However, as we have already seen, Heidegger understands Dasein's opening up of its world as an event that precedes the distinction between passivity and activity. The opening up of the world is something that at once happens to Dasein and that it does. That the world is *disclosed* means that in a certain sense its potential meaning is already there. It is in interpretation that Dasein brings some of the potential significance of its world into view. The disclosure of the world that must precede any such laying bare of potential meanings is what makes those meanings possible for the Dasein in the first place and allows them to be 'there' for it. In the same way, *projection* must not here be understood in the sense used when we say, for example, 'He is projecting his own feelings onto this situation.' There is not a world of bare items or objects standing around which Dasein then 'projects' possible meanings onto and calls that its world. Rather, in projecting, Dasein opens its world and brings possible meanings into being. Within that world it is then one possibility that 'items' or 'objects' will lose their meaning and come to be discovered as just standing around without meaning. A further possibility is that I then 'project' arbitrary feelings and meanings onto such items, but that kind of projection is strictly secondary to the projecting open of a world in the first place.

To say that the projective-disclosure of the world is in some sense prior to Dasein's ability to be in a world of possible meanings, does not mean that this takes place once and for all at any particular point and that after that all possible meanings are fixed and we simply have to get on with making our way within that world. So long as Dasein is, it is opening up its world. The contours of that world shift and change all the time as Dasein negotiates the world of possibilities that it has already opened up. The world is always finite, but that does not mean that it has a fixed boundary. It is misleading even to suggest that the world has a boundary in the usual sense, since we cannot make sense of anything being beyond such a boundary. The world of possible meaning is thus not like my conscious awareness, the finitude of which is obvious because there is clearly something beyond it, that is, a whole world of things that I can possibly be aware of. The world encompasses all my possibilities including my possibilities for awareness. Heidegger often uses the idea of an 'horizon' to designate the sense in which the world is finite. I am not consciously aware of everything up to the horizon, but the horizon *encompasses* and encloses everything which I can be consciously aware of or that we can understand in its involvements. Yet we should not let this notion mislead us into thinking that there is something beyond the 'horizon' of the world that is already there waiting to come within the field of possible meanings, as that which is over the horizon in the field of vision is already there waiting to be brought within its compass. We usually understand horizon in terms of the field of vision, but a field of vision is actually only a possibility that is encompassed within a world that is projected open: 'We understand "horizon" to be the circumference of the field of vision. But horizon, from *horizein*, is not at all primarily related to looking and intuiting, but by itself means simply that which delimits, encloses, the *enclosure*.'[13] The most important thing about the horizonal character of the world is that within the horizon a world is disclosed, but that disclosure itself is enclosed and delimits itself. When the world of possible meanings is projected open and disclosed by Dasein, this is always at the same time a delimitation of what is possible for it and what it can understand or fail to understand. It is this projective-disclosure of the world, the opening up of the world that is also the delimitation and enclosure of the world, that Heidegger thinks of as truth.

### iii. DECISIVE TRUTHS

Truth thus encompasses far more than assertions or judgments and whether or not they are adequate representations of isolated states of affairs. We can begin to see that the scope of truth is far greater than the usual focus on propositional truth suggests, if we recall that we call many things 'true' that are not assertions. We speak of 'true' gold in the sense of 'genuine' or 'real' gold.[14] Clearly what is involved in an assertion being true is very different from what is involved in something like gold being genuine. Nevertheless, Heidegger argues that we should not be deceived into thinking that truth is primarily a property belonging to certain assertions and that it is in assertions that we find the 'true' locus of truth, while the truth of anything else is derived from propositional truth. Neither should we think that the different kinds of truth that we come across are utterly disparate phenomena. They all receive their character as true or false, genuine or fake, from Dasein's encompassing disclosure of the world. An assertion is correct or incorrect in laying bare one or more of the possible meanings of the world that Dasein has projected open. Gold is 'genuine' or 'fake' because Dasein has projected open a world in which one physical element is involved in various possibilities that others are not. It is the disclosure of the world that is the proper 'locus' of truth.

The encompassing disclosure of possible meanings is what allows for any assertion to be correct or incorrect, any item to be 'genuine' or 'fake', any behavior to be truthful or misleading. Dasein's world discloses and encompasses all statements that are correct and incorrect, all genuine and fake items and all behavior that is truthful or misleading. Yet the way that Dasein discloses its world can itself also be more or less genuine or 'truthful'. Dasein can exist in such a way that it distinguishes between an authentic and inauthentic disclosure of the world. We can gain a preliminary understanding of what this means in the idea of being true to ourselves. Generally speaking, to be true to ourselves means to hold to our principles and convictions. Principles and convictions are what has been decided upon already and then made applicable to the ways we comport ourselves towards people and things within the world. These are the principles and convictions that 'one' has decided upon. For Heidegger, however, to hold convictions is not simply to follow the guidelines that have been laid down for us and that we have laid down for ourselves as part of the One. It is to *resolve* to follow them or to challenge them so as to be truly oneself in each case. That kind of resolution can never be made once and for all, but must be renewed in each case. Heidegger calls the kind of disclosure in which Dasein is true to itself, and is thus able to hold principles and convictions, 'resolute disclosure'.[15]

Most of the time we simply rely on principles and convictions that have already been put in place. In fact, we cannot do otherwise. It is in the 'One' that particular principles and convictions have their root. In resolute disclosure Dasein does not wipe all of this out and build an entirely new set of principles from scratch. Nor does it simply surrender itself to the way that One has interpreted things. Nor again is it a question of picking and choosing from what one has already interpreted and articulated as possibilities, taking up some of it and leaving the rest to one side. In resolute disclosure Dasein comports itself to all of the possibilities that have been laid out already, to all of those that have been forgotten or lost and to what may be otherwise and it *opens* the world for itself in a resolution that is open to other possibilities.

Resolute disclosure does not mean that I can simply decide what is true, in the sense of what is factually the case. It is never open to us to simply choose which assertions are correct and which are incorrect. In scientific inquiry, for example, resolute disclosure means that there is a set of principles and convictions that one has decided upon and which those engaging in this type of inquiry are committed to. Those convictions are to do with how we should go about conducting this kind of inquiry, the methods to be adopted, what is to count as a result for the inquiry, what should be disregarded as irrelevant or not within the scope of inquiry. Resoluteness in scientific inquiry is to be committed to those convictions in a way that may show that the 'correct' procedure needs to be revised. Resolution is not something over and on top of commitment; it is the holding to a commitment for the sake of disclosure, rather than for its own sake. Resolute disclosure in this case is the resolution of a scientist to open these commitments to what is disclosed by and through acting upon them. That resolution can be essential to scientific inquiry of any kind. In certain circumstances it may solicit great heroism and courage from the scientists who resolutely disclose the world by means of them.

Scientific inquiry is, however, not the only kind of disclosure that can be resolute or not. It is commonplace that in scientific inquiry conviction is the enemy of truth and it is certainly the case that science ideally strives against any prior conviction as to what actually is the case, that is, what the facts of the matter are. Yet Heidegger follows in Nietzsche's footsteps with the claim that whilst scientific inquiry combats all kinds of dogmatic assertions about what is factually the case, it is grounded in a deeper kind of conviction of its own. As Nietzsche puts it:

> *To make it possible for the discipline to begin*, must there not be some prior conviction – even one that is so commanding and unconditional that it sacrifices all other convictions to itself? We see that science also rests on faith; there is simply no science "without presuppositions." The question of whether *truth* is needed must not only have been affirmed in advance, but affirmed to such a degree that the principle, the faith, the conviction finds expression: "*Nothing* is needed *more* than truth, and in relation to that everything else has only a second-rate value."[16]

Nietzsche suggests that the resolution or 'faith' that underlies all science is a commitment to 'truth itself', which implies that any other commitment can have nothing to do with truth. Heidegger, on the other hand, argues that truth is not only scientific truth. The critique of scientific truth that Heidegger shares with Nietzsche does not involve disparaging the commitments of science, nor does it claim that there is no truth there. On the contrary, both of these thinkers respected the resolute disclosure of the world that scientific inquiry can bring about. Their critique is of the tendency to regard the commitments and convictions of scientific inquiry as the only commitments that are worth making and the truths they disclose as the only truths there can be. Heidegger regarded the scientific disclosure of the world as *one* way in which the world can be disclosed and the convictions through which that disclosure takes place as an important but non-exclusive set of commitments that do not simply have self-evident priority. As he puts it in *The Fundamental Concepts of Metaphysics*: 'What is at issue here is not the opposition between actual reality and illusory appearance, but the distinction between quite different *kinds* of possible *truth*'.[17] There he names *myth* and *art* as ways of truth, ways of disclosing possibilities, alongside scientific truth. We must not allow ourselves to be prematurely persuaded that scientific investigation is the only way of truth that is committed to principles that uncover the world and yet is open to the questioning of those principles in the light of what is uncovered. It is the unquestioning commitment to *that one way* of disclosing as being the only way, that can become the 'faith' of science, a faith that Heidegger sought to bring into question.

### iv. EXCAVATING AND SHELTERING THE TRUTH

In *Being and Time* Heidegger argues that 'Dasein is in the truth'.[18] This does not mean that we have a general tendency to make correct assertions and only occasionally make mistakes. Nor does it mean that we have a general tendency to be honest and only occasionally tell lies. What it means is that we project open a world of meaning and in doing so we are able to be committed to truth and make the truth manifest. It also entails that in and through its being 'in the truth' Dasein is also in 'untruth'.[19] That means that we become oblivious to the projecting open of this world of meaning, along with the convictions and potential commitments that go into that projection, because we are absorbed and engaged in the world that is already opened up for us.

Truth, according to *Being and Time* is disclosure, since Dasein is able to discover things in and about the world because it discloses the world to itself.[20] Yet it is only by disclosing itself that Dasein can discover the world and by discovering the world disclose itself. Disclosure and discovery are thus facets of the basic phenomenon of truth that Heidegger calls in *Being and Time* 'uncoveredness' (*Entdecktheit*): ' "Being-true" ("truth") is Being-uncovering.'[21] Heidegger will also call the basic phenomenon of truth 'unveiling' (*Enthüllen*)[22] and 'unconcealment' (*Unverborgenheit*). All of these terms for 'primordial truth' are attempted translations of what was called in Greek *alētheia*, a word usually translated as 'truth'. What is important for Heidegger about the Greek understanding of truth is that it is not some static state or a property that belongs to any items, but something that occurs or takes place. What takes place is the taking away of what covers over, veils or conceals. The 'a' at the beginning of the Greek word denoted a lack or privation and *lēthe*, what is forgotten, meaning for Heidegger what is covered over or concealed. So the Greek conception of truth was the taking away of that which covers, veils or conceals. All of Heidegger's translations mirror the structure of the Greek term, with the 'un' at the beginning indicating the removal of the cover, veil or concealment. The Greek concept of truth thus has the potential to indicate to us what Heidegger at this point thinks of as the most basic phenomenon of truth. It is uncovering that reveals Dasein and its world of possible meanings to itself and is the condition for all truths and falsehoods, whether that be the making of correct or incorrect assertions, honest or dishonest behavior or the discovery of genuine or fake gold.

The Greek conception of truth as uncovering, unveiling or unconcealing is of great significance to Heidegger, but it would be a mistake to say that he calls us to go back to an ancient understanding of truth as 'unconcealment'. This is because he did not think that there was one 'theory of truth' that was shared by all the Greeks. The Greeks had vastly differing interpretations of what this 'unconcealing' involves and Heidegger often suggests that they did not manage to provide an adequate interpretation of it. All that 'unconcealment' provides us with is a clue to understanding that truth is best thought of not as value or property of an item, but as the unconcealing of a world of possible significance.

It would also be an error to say that Heidegger claims we should return to the Greek thinking of truth as 'unconcealment', because he comes to think that there was a distortion of the basic phenomenon of truth initiated in Greek thinking. In essence, Heidegger later argues that in the Greek thinking of truth the emphasis is always on the first element, on the *a-* of privation. Truth was always *un*covering, *un*veiling or *un*concealment. As Heidegger puts it in a manuscript from the late 1930s, *Contributions to Philosophy (from Enowning)*:

> a-lētheia means unconcealment and the unconcealed itself. This already shows that concealing itself is only experienced as what is to be *abolished*, what is to be taken away (a-).[23]

In *Being and Time* Heidegger himself also emphasizes the *un*coveredness of truth. In the case of making factual discoveries within the world, he remarks that, 'Beings need to be snatched out of their hiddenness. The factical uncoveredness of anything is always, as it were, a kind of *robbery*'.[24] This emphasis on the *un*covering manifests itself in the *dis*covery of facts and *dis*closure of ourselves. This emphasis on *un*covering set the course for the history of our thinking about truth. It has eventually led to a culture whose impossible ideal is that everything within the horizon of possible meaning should be completely clarified and within view. The over-emphasis on *dis*covery and *dis*closure, stemming from the thinking of truth as *un*concealment, leads to a distorted way of inhabiting the world, because it sees *all* concealment, not just that involved in incorrect assertions and dishonest dealings, as that which would ideally be done away with completely.

We might call this way of thinking about the basic phenomenon of truth and the way of inhabiting the world that accompanies it the *excavation* of truth. Such a designation should remind us of the allegory of the cave in Plato's *Republic*, book 7, in which Heidegger thought we find one of the most important interpretations of truth in the tradition. The allegory tells of prisoners who are chained within a cave in a world of illusions and shadows projected onto the walls of the cave and the various stages of liberation which a prisoner might pass through before reaching the open world and eventually seeing the sun, which was all along the source of what was revealed, even in illusion. Heidegger undertook several extended readings of this allegory. In 'Plato's Doctrine of Truth' an essay from 1940 in which these readings culminate, he emphasizes the way that there is 'unconcealment' at every stage even in illusion. So Dasein is 'in the truth' already and what is at stake is liberation into the 'most unhidden'. Again, truth is achieved in a positive taking away: 'The unhidden must be torn from a hiddenness; it must in a sense be stolen from hiddenness.'[25] Heidegger argues that

Plato already moves us away from this understanding of truth towards truth as what is purely present in the *idea* or form of things. This then precipitates the whole history of thought about truth understood primarily as correctness.[26] Nevertheless, that change in truth that took place with Plato is still rooted in the *un*covering of truth, in its excavation.

Heidegger continued to think that we need to return to the sense of truth not as having a correct view of what is purely present, but as an uncovering that takes place in and through Dasein's way of being. Yet he also slowly begins to develop the thought that there has always been an emphasis on the uncovering, while that uncovering is always also involved in covering over. He therefore tries to re-emphasize the other pole of truth, that in excavation is the negative covering, veiling or concealing. Covering is implicit in the uncovering, but already on its way to obliteration in truth thought only in terms of its removal. This does not in the least entail that we should cease trying to make discoveries and retreat into obscurantism and occultism, any more than it means we should cease trying to be 'truthful', open and honest in our behavior. It does entail that we should begin to think of what we are doing in understanding, clarifying, discovering and disclosing as something that takes place within the horizon of possible meaning that encloses as it discloses. The world of possible meaning will then no longer be thought of as something that could ideally be completely disclosed and given a final shape. The world of what is possible and intelligible as it is opened, conceals other ways in which that opening could take place and thus other realms of possibility.

Heidegger tries a number of ways to express this and to initiate a shift in our thinking of truth as unconcealment. He introduces the concept of 'earth' in lectures from 1935 entitled 'The Origin of the Work of Art', as that which is brought forth in a world but never fully disclosed in any disclosure: 'The earth is openly illuminated as itself only where it is apprehended and preserved as the essentially undisclosable, as that which withdraws from every disclosure, in other words, keeps itself constantly closed up.'[27] The earth, as Heidegger understands it, is not a thing that appears in the world, such as one planet in the solar system. Rather it refers to what is never fully present within the horizon of possibilities and potential significance that makes up the world. Just as there is a world of potential significance wherever Dasein exists, the earth is that which comes forth in but at the same time always escapes the world. The earth itself is beyond all horizons of possibility, yet it is the earth that allows for the formation and manifestation of the world. Truth no longer simply discloses a world but at the same time returns to the concealment of the earth.

Truth might then not simply be 'robbery' and 'tearing' of what is hidden into unhiddenness, but the transformation of covering into a sheltering and preserving of what allows for the opening of a world. Heidegger's understanding of the 'covering' in truth comes to reflect the truth of preservation that remained concealed in the Greek understanding of truth. We can begin to think of that covering as sheltering or preserving (*Bergung*): 'Sheltering of truth as growing back into closedness of the earth'.[28] Within our present understanding of truth it only makes sense to preserve possibilities that have been excavated and disclosed or that which is being held in reserve for excavation. Within the truth that Heidegger hopes to initiate, preservation of the earth would be undertaken in the very manner that we open up and inhabit the world.

# CHAPTER 7

# TIME AND SPACE

Time and space come into being together and are therefore probably one, like subject and object.

*General Draft*, 41

We begin to measure space and time in a multitude of ways. We measure our height and the changes in our height as we grow, against the door frame. We measure the width of a tree by trying to encircle it with our arms. We measure the distance home by trying to run back before anyone notices we were gone. We measure the time until we have to go to bed in terms of how much more of a story can be told.

Later we learn more formal ways of measuring. We are taught to measure space using a ruler and other equipment. There are generally accepted units of measurement, meters and centimeters or feet and inches. Space becomes what we measure with a ruler. It becomes something composed of lines and points and the measurement of space comes to involve picking out sections of those lines. We set up a grid of intersecting lines against which to measure distances. Eventually this grid becomes, to a large extent, the space that we inhabit. Similarly, we are taught to measure time using clocks and watches. Time too is given its standard units of measurement, hours, minutes and seconds. Time becomes that which we measure using clocks. We also learn to use 'timelines' to plot the course of time, whether it be on a large or relatively small scale. Time becomes a vastly extended and perhaps endless line. Measuring time becomes the picking out of sections of this line. Eventually this line becomes, to a large extent, the time that we inhabit.

Of course, we also continue to measure space and time in the multitude of less formal ways that we did before. However, the inculcation of 'ruler-space' and 'clock-time'[1] is thorough enough for us to begin to think that these formal measurements are the only real ways of measuring space and time. We think that formal measurement gets us closer to what space and time 'really are', while informal measurements are nothing but rough approximations that could be done better formally. The justification given for this view is that formal measurement affords us abilities, ways of negotiating and getting on in the world that informal measurement does not. The 'ability-to-be' that informal measurements afford us is simply taken for granted and assumed to be insignificant.

A number of metaphysical problems arise with the institution of 'ruler-space' and 'clock-time'. Is the grid of lines that we come to think of as space itself actually 'out there' in the world, or is it 'just in my head'? Does it have objective reality or is it only subjective? Is the line of time in the world or in me? Since the time that I experience is not generally like a continuous line, are there perhaps two times, subjective and objective? Are the lines of the grid of space and the line of time continuous or are they made up of discrete points? These are precisely the kinds of question that metaphysicians have grappled with, especially after scientific mathematization made formalization of space and time almost ubiquitous. Significantly, the everyday space and time that we now inhabit involve a good deal of formalized measurement. That semi-formalized everyday space and time even become a hindrance to further scientific formalization. The kinds of measurement of space-time that take place in modern physics, in which any dimension can be measured against any other and space and time themselves can 'bend', are very hard if not impossible for everyday understanding to accept.

For Heidegger the metaphysical questions that arise concerning space and time as they are measured in any of these ways cannot be given a satisfactory answer in the form in which they are posed. Space and time are not originally things, whether things 'out there' in the world or 'in my head'. Space and time are what take place when Dasein is in the world. Space and time are ways in which Dasein's world is opened up. In *Being and Time* Heidegger argues that *time*, or the way in which time is 'temporalized', is the most basic way in which such opening up takes place. So the question to ask, in accordance with the phenomenological way of proceeding,

is not *what* space and time are, but *how* do they take place? How is
space spatialized and time temporalized?

## i. EXTENDING OUR REACH AND MAKING ROOM

Dasein is able to locate things in space, including its own body, but
Dasein itself is not located in space. It is Dasein's 'spatializing'
that brings about the space in which anything can be positioned,
whether it be in terms of formally delineated positions or less
determinate rough locations. This includes any positioning or rough
localization of its own body. To understand the phenomenon of
space we need to try to characterize how this spatialization occurs.
The two central characteristics of spatialization that Heidegger
points us towards in *Being and Time* are 'de-severence' and 'directionality'.[2] The term translated as 'de-severence' is derived by
Heidegger from the everyday word '*Entfernung*', that can mean
distance and space. By hyphenating this word to make '*Ent-fernung*'
Heidegger draws attention to the prefix 'Ent', to take away or
abolish, and the stem 'Ferne', distance: ' "De-severing" amounts to
making the farness vanish – that is, making the remoteness of something disappear, bringing it close.'[3] This does not mean that in its
spatializing Dasein is always taking some determinately measured
distance, say the length of a meter, and then trying to reduce it,
perhaps by cutting it into two half meters. Rather, what it means is
that we are always trying to bring what surrounds us within reach.
Distances are primarily experienced as what is to be overcome to get
things within reach.

If de-severence means 'getting within reach', what exactly does
that mean? If it is to existentially characterize the way that Dasein
spatializes space, it cannot mean simply gathering as many items or
objects within arm's length as possible. Rather, having something
within arm's length, so that I do not have to walk across the room
to touch it, but can simply reach out my arm, is one particular
instance of getting things within reach. The rough distance 'within
arm's length' is a distance that comes into being in particular kinds
of 'de-severence', or getting things within reach. Primarily it is
the 'ready-to-hand' equipment or tackle of the surrounding world
that Dasein gets within its reach. There are prominent instances of
de-severence all around us. A remote control brings the TV within
reach without needing to bring the actual set within arm's length.

Communications technologies allow us to be 'in touch' with others, to be able to reach them, without the remotest possibility of coming into physical contact with them. Yet we cover the distance. It is the extent and power of our 'reach' that give 'near' and 'far' their everyday meanings. A distance of one mile from where I am now standing is neither near nor far. It is near if it can be covered with ease, say if I'm fit and healthy and about to walk it at a good pace. It is impossibly far if I have only just got to my feet after a long illness, or have been walking solidly in the blazing sun all day. The formal measuring out of a distance as 'one mile' takes place within an engagement with the environing world which entails that this measurement will mean near or far in terms of what Dasein is bringing within reach. The mile does not lie there waiting to be thought of as near or far; it is measured out by Dasein, for whom it has the character of near or far as it measures.

The other basic characteristic of Dasein's spatialization that Heidegger points out in *Being and Time* is 'directionality'.[4] This characteristic is already there in de-severence. In bringing things within reach I am directionally orientated. I am flying away from London and towards New York. I am going up or down stairs. I am running towards the finish line or away from the dog. If we think of a completely formalized space then it appears to have neither direction nor orientation in itself. It appears that people orientate themselves in space that itself has no orientation. In fact, Dasein projects open such a formalized space in order to aid the orientatation of itself in ways that do not come naturally to it. A map is a partial formalization of space, a space that itself is not going in one direction or another, but which allows Dasein to orientate itself in ways that it could not otherwise. In its directional orientation in space Dasein 'articulates' space,[5] which here means it divides space into regions. Dasein is generally thrown into particular articulations, but there is nothing 'natural' or immutable about any particular articulation and regionalization of space. Nevertheless, Dasein has always articulated space on one way or another. This articulation allows for everything from the division of houses into levels and rooms to the division of terrain into countries and counties, or even the division of outer space into galaxies and solar systems.

Through the de-severence by which it extends its reach and the directionality by which it orientates itself Dasein 'makes room'.[6] It clears a space for things to take their place. Most of the time in our everyday lives, we clear a space for the equipmental 'tackle' and furniture of our familiar world. Making space of some kind is essential for 'ready-to-hand' equipment to run smoothly. If things 'press in' on us too much then there is no space for them to work well. We need to clear a space in order to have them properly within our reach. A TV screen, for example, is 'ready-to-hand' and working well if it is at a fair distance. If it is right in front of my nose, where I can reach out and touch it with my hand, it is actually working less well and is less 'ready-to-hand'. A pen, on the other hand, is no good at all unless I can reach it with my hand. Things work best when they have their place, that is, a place in which Dasein has them ready-to-hand. In making room Dasein gives them their place. This is why Heidegger claims in *Being and Time* that: 'This "giving space", which is also "*making room*" for them, consists in freeing the ready-to-hand for its spatiality.'[7] 'Making room' is also carried over into our organization of time when we say that we will 'make room' in our schedule or 'clear a space in my diary'.

Since we are generally completely caught up in the management and organization of ready-to-hand equipment, making room for it, or giving it space to run smoothly, this is the way that we make room for ourselves. However, Heidegger later begins to question whether 'making room' for equipment is the most fundamental way in which spatialization takes place. The extent and power of our 'reach' has in many ways been increasing enormously. This is a phenomenon that Heidegger continues to reflect on for many years after *Being and Time*. His 1950 essay 'The Thing', for example, considers what it is for things to be near to us and begins by pointing to the increasing strength and power of our reach: 'All distances in time and space are shrinking. Man reaches overnight, by plane, places which formerly took weeks and months to travel.'[8] The measured distances are not reduced, but as our reach can cover them with greater and greater ease their character is changed. The determinate distances of outer space, for example, are huge. Yet in some ways we now have galaxies quite comfortably within our reach that a while ago were completely beyond it. We can see them, photograph them, and use light that reaches us from them to measure formally a great many different distances in space and time. In other ways, of course, such as the possibility of bringing our bodies within proximity of them, they are still completely beyond our reach. In 'The Thing' Heidegger goes on to consider whether the 'de-severence' that takes place as the extension of reach really is what makes things 'near' to us. De-severence as it is analyzed in *Being and Time* may be the root of the everyday sense in which we try to bring things near to us by getting them 'within reach', but the question that Heidegger raises now is whether space is ultimately a question of finding distances in the attempt to overcome them. Perhaps spatialization involves becoming acquainted with what is around us not simply in terms of getting it within reach by overcoming distance. Perhaps there are ways of clearing space and making room for ourselves that are more important and more essential than those manifested in extending our reach and organizing everything to run as smoothly as possible. Is it not at least possible that the continuous extension of our reach can cover over the necessity of clearing a space for ourselves that we are able to inhabit?

## ii. EXPLODING, STRETCHING AND PUNCTUATING TIME

Time is clearly the keystone to Heidegger's phenomenological project in *Being and Time*. He writes in the preface to this treatise: 'Our provisional aim is the interpretation of *time* as the possible horizon of any understanding whatsoever of being.'[9] In other words, being is to be interpreted *as* time. This does not mean, as we can now start to appreciate, that despite appearances all the different kinds of items and objects within the world are really some special kind of thing or substance called time. It means that Heidegger interprets time as the fundamental way in which Dasein opens up a world of possible meanings. Time is the temporalization that discloses and encloses Dasein's world.

There were a number of very important precedents for Heidegger's focus on time as the fundamental way in which phenomena are opened up. First of all, time was of central importance in Immanuel Kant's thinking of phenomenal appearance. In the *Critique of Pure Reason* Kant had argued that time is in us, in the fundamental sense that it is a 'form of intuition' given by the subject to its world.[10] Nevertheless, time does not belong primarily to subjective appearances. The time series of subjective appearances depends upon the time series of objective appearances and Kant thought that by showing this to be the case he could overcome skepticism about the 'external' world.[11] Yet this was not what

Heidegger ultimately found to be of central importance in Kant's thinking of time. Rather it was the necessity that pure concepts or 'categories' be made temporal or 'schematized'[12] in order to apply to the intuitions that we receive, that suggested to Heidegger that Kant was on the way to thinking of temporalization itself as the fundamental event in which both subjective and objective experience occurs. In other words, perhaps time is another name of the 'transcendental power of imagination' that, as we saw in Chapter 1, Heidegger interprets as the root source of Kant's distinct 'faculties' of intuition and cognition.

Henri Bergson, a very influential French philosopher at the end of the nineteenth and beginning of the twentieth century, agreed with Kant on the key significance of time. However, Bergson also criticized Kant on a number of points. First, he did not think that time belonged primarily to the subject in any sense, but neither was it objectively within the world. Time, for Bergson, is a pure activity that he often simply called 'life', and objectification was something that took place within this activity. Secondly, Bergson argues that Kant is wrong to think of time as a *homogeneous series*. The 'line' of time is a 'spatialization' of time, while time itself is composed of 'durations' that differ in quality not just quantity.[13] What Bergson calls 'spatialization' is the result of what we called above 'formalized measurement'. Yet Bergson thought that spatialization is particularly bound up with the possibility of mathematical formalization, while time itself as duration will always escape such representations. His position is in many ways close to Heidegger's in *Being and Time*, since they both think that temporalization is the fundamental way, prior to the distinction between subject and object, in which things come into being.[14] However, Heidegger does not think that spatialization is any more or less apt for formalization than temporalization. Both space and time can be formalized and thought of as an item, such as a line, but neither is primordially objectified.

Finally, Edmund Husserl came to think of the phenomenological analysis of time as essential for filling out how it is that consciousness is 'intentionally' directed. In a series of lectures he delivered in 1905 entitled 'The Phenomenology of Internal Time Consciousness',[15] Husserl argued that time was a basic way in which consciousness constitutes its world, prior to the intellectualized forms of 'higher' consciousness that seek to cognize and gain theoretical knowledge of the world. If we look at how we are actually conscious of time as a primary intentionality, we see that presence in time is not a vanishing and momentary 'now-point' but as an extended presence in which the past and future are always implicated. Analyzing the lived experience of listening to a melody, Husserl describes the way in which hearing a note is always affected by what has come before and what is to come after. In every presence there is retention of what has come before and protention of what is to come. This does not mean that we always actively remember what has gone before or that we recall what comes next from last time we heard this piece, having to guess what follows if we have not heard it before. Retention and protention as Husserl understands them mean that any presence in time is an expanding stretch into the past and future. Experiences are not things that take place in time and no experience has a determinate length that can be measured, but is itself the temporalization of time as an expansion of presence.

Heidegger's interpretation of how temporalization takes place as the opening up of the world retains a great deal from each of these analyses but also moves beyond them all. The claim of *Being and Time* is that a fundamental analysis of temporalization will allow us to properly interpret how Dasein opens up a world of possible meanings for itself, how it is 'in the truth' as a being that 'cares', that is, how it exists in the world. The crucial characteristic of temporalization for Heidegger is that it is *ecstatic*. He calls his interpretation of temporalization 'ecstatic temporality'. This means, in accordance with the etymology of the Greek term, that in temporalization time always *stands outside* of itself: '*Temporality is the primordial "outside-of-itself" in and for itself*. We therefore call the phenomena of the future, the character of having been, and the Present, the "*ecstases*" of temporality.'[16] Each dimension of time, past, present and future, stands outside of itself and in the midst of the others where it encounters itself. Each of the 'ecstases' of time is shot through with the others. Past, present and future explode into one another. In doing so they do not disperse completely but encounter one another and are unified. So we must cease to think of time even as an expanding present encompassing past and future. 'The present' is not more fully present and manifest than the past or the future. Becoming present and disappearing constantly take place in the field opened up by the explosion of the dimensions of time into one another.

One consequence of this 'ecstatic' understanding of temporality is that time is not fundamentally in a subject, nor is it some item or occurrence within the world.[17] We cannot begin with 'inner time' and then see objective 'outer time' as a particular way in which that time manifests itself. Nor can we begin with time as an occurrence within the world and see subjective experience as something that takes place within that time. Time is the throwing open of a world. Dasein is outside of itself 'in the world' because it *is* the temporalization that is always outside of itself. As a consequence Dasein's intentionality does not move from inside to outside; it is already outside in the world.

Temporalization is thus the fundamental event that opens up a world of meaning. Temporalization is the meaning of 'Care', the way of being that belongs to Dasein in its opening up of the world. This does not mean that Care takes place 'in time', but rather that Care takes place as temporalization. Dasein cares for what is to come and is ahead-of-itself (future); it is thrown into a world as already-being-in (past as 'having been') and it is alongside things in the world as 'being-alongside' (present).[18] Dasein as the opening up of the world does so in each of these modes not in a series, one after another, but also not in a timeless instant. The three 'ecstases' of time take place as the unified way that Dasein is open to the world. There could be no opening of a world if the ecstases of temporalization were required to follow one another in sequence. In fact, in opposition to the strongest tendencies of everyday and metaphysical thought, that usually assigns 'reality' primarily to the present 'now', then to the past because it 'was once present' and finally to the future because it 'is not yet', but will be present, Heidegger assigns priority to the future.[19]

How could that be? The future is what is not yet, but which is to come and it is with an orientation to what is to come that Dasein cares about the past and the present. We can begin to understand this when we see that our engagements with the world always take place for the sake of the future. Even when we are conducting historical research into the depths of the past, even when we are thinking about the origins of life, or the origins of the stars or the origins of the universe, we do so for the sake of the future. The future I am concerned with may only be the future possibilities of gaining further understanding of the past, but it is always with regard to the future that we engage with anything. In engaging with the equipment and the others that are around me I can do so on the basis of the meaningful possibilities that have been put in place, but again I am open to what has been put in place and what it means in the present through an orientation towards what is to come. It may be that Dasein has a relatively closed orientation towards the future, open only towards its personal and immediate possibilities, or the possibilities of continuing in certain ways as before. On the other hand, Dasein can be open to what is to come for future generations, whole communities, humanity or life itself. It may be orientated towards what is to come in a way that is open to possibilities that have not already been put in place. That is, it may be trying to find new ways of going about things. In each case, it is from openness to the future that the past and the present are themselves opened up.

Together with the ecstatic character of time that is opened towards the future, Heidegger also sees temporalization as involving time's *stretching itself out*. It is this characteristic that accounts for the generation of our ordinary concepts of time from ecstatic temporality. In looking towards the future we stretch ourselves out as meaningful stretches of time, or what we call in everyday terms 'experiences' when referring to a personal 'life span', and 'occurrences' when referring to the span of a communal life. Since Dasein is not originally separated from others, these can only name two aspects of the same stretching of time. The stretching out of a life time, both personal and communal, is what Heidegger calls 'historizing' and the existentiale that belongs to Dasein because it stretches out time in this way is called 'historicality'. In its historicality, 'Dasein *is stretched along and stretches itself along* [. . .].'[20] The historizing that belongs to Dasein's temporalization is the source of our 'ordinary' concept of time as a series in which one thing follows another. Time is stretched out and becomes a 'road' and the 'flow of a river' or eventually simply a line. On the whole these ways of speaking mislead us into thinking that time *is* a road, a flow or a line. Temporalization itself, however, is not a being, occurrence or movement at all, since all beings and their movements occur in a world that is opened up through temporalization.

Finally, if temporalization *is* Dasein's existence we should be able to characterize the difference within existence, between the authentic and inauthentic, in terms of temporalization. Heidegger does this by integrating two very different concepts of time from the philosophical tradition into one unified understanding of temporalization. The Greeks spoke of time in two different ways. *Chronos* meant time, but also a certain stretch of time like a day or a season. Our term chronology, meaning a correctly ordered series, is derived from *chronos*. However, for Heidegger, chronology is just a way of formally ordering the stretches of time that Dasein stretches out as it historizes time. Chronos is the result of historized temporalization, that is, the stretches of time that result from time stretching itself along and being stretched along. Aristotle gave the classic analysis of *chronos* in book 4 of *Physics*, and Heidegger translates his definition as, 'that which is counted in the movement which we encounter within the horizon of earlier and later.'[21] This concept of time is derived from a concern to measure stretches or spans of time that we are trying to deal with in everyday concerned dealings, when we tend to think of time as a sequence of nows. Heidegger offers a critique of this and all conceptions of time that view time as a sequence of nows, claiming not that they are wrong or incorrect, but that they aim to tell us about the stretches of time that result from historizing temporalization and thus cover over the original temporalization that gave rise to those stretches. So chronological time is time that is already stretched out and has been made available for formal ordering.

The other Greek term for time is *kairos*. This designates the right time for action or the critical moment. Aristotle also gives an analysis of *kairos*, in his writings on ethics and rhetoric.[22] Kairos is what we might describe as time that is *meaningfully punctuated*. It is time as seen in what Heidegger calls a 'moment of vision'. The moment of vision is not something that happens in time and it cannot be understood in terms of nows.[23] It is nothing other than the ecstatic temporality that stretches itself out in authentic temporalizing. The principal modern forerunners of the thinking of *kairos*, or the 'moment of vision', are once more Kierkegaard and Nietzsche.[24] For Heidegger, the distinguishing feature of his own thinking of authentic temporality is that these two times, *chronos* as the time that has stretched itself out and *kairos* as meaningfully punctuated time, are modifications of our unified temporalizing, not dissociated times. *Kairos* is authentic *chronos*. Dasein stretches out time in a moment of vision, but in that stretching it tends to become absorbed in the stretches, in the 'experiences' and 'events' that it is stretching out. These stretches of time can lose their significance and become formally empty sequences of nows. However, Dasein can also exist in such a way that it stretches out its time again and again with the original significance that comes in the moment of vision. *Chronos and kairos* are often dissociated, the former being understood as time seen from a theoretical standpoint and the latter as time seen from a practical standpoint. Heidegger argues that we need to see the two as modes of the same fundamental temporalization. Dissociation is a way of leaving Dasein's existence undifferentiated.

How should we understand the difference between these modes of temporalization? We have a tendency to think that time is 'really' a meaningless stretch or expanse, or perhaps a number of stretches and expanses. That is objective time. Then we subjectively find meaning in or impose meaning onto those stretches. For Heidegger, original temporalization can be said to be 'more' subjective than any subject, because it makes any factically existing self possible, but also 'more' objective than any object, because it is the condition for any object being 'there'.[25] ' "Time" is present-at-hand neither in the subject nor in the "Object", neither "inside" nor "outside"; it "is" *"earlier"* than any subjectivity or Objectivity, because it presents the condition for the very possibility of this "earlier".'[26] Prior to objective and subjective times there is time as a temporalization that is outside of itself and stretches itself out. Those stretches are already significant. The 'moment of vision' is not something removed from time or interrupting time; it is the return to that original significance of the ecstatic stretching. We are originally 'in the moment', in 'significant' times in our personal, communal and historical existence. A career crisis, or falling in love or facing a moral dilemma are not originally things that happen in stretches of time, but are stretched out in original temporalization as significant for the future. The 'turning points' in history, such as the Fall of the Roman Empire or the French Revolution, are themselves not events that happen in a homogeneous sequence of time, but were and are stretched by Dasein from out of its future possibilities. We might then ask, how long do these 'moments' last? They are not timeless instants, but neither are they of determinate length. One can more or less arbitrarily date the beginning and the end events chronologically when the event is supposed to be 'over and done with'. But the history of the French Revolution could be indefinitely stretched backwards in the 'build up'. Furthermore, it is stretched out from the future that is yet to come for any Dasein who is open to it, so that it is never finally 'over and done with'. There is more to come in terms of our knowledge of this event, but also in terms of what this event will mean for us in the future. There are no 'natural' break-off points, there is just the stretch that Dasein makes of itself. Primordially the stretching of time is always a 'turning point in history' or a 'significant' moment for Dasein. One might object that this may or may not be the case for the stretch of time that covers Dasein's history, but there were enormous 'stretches' of time in which there was no Dasein. Heidegger's thought is that insofar as time is stretched open by and for Dasein then it originally has significance, although this may simply be in terms of our future possibilities for knowing about and understanding a past in which there was no Dasein.

Temporalization in the moment of vision is a call to 'take action', hence the traditional understanding of *kairos* as the right time for action. This is because in this temporalization the 'ultimate' significance of its stretching of time is always yet to come. The whole meaning, duration and intelligible possibilities that belong to a stretch that is understood chronologically to be over and done with, can be transformed in what is yet to come. In the moment of vision Dasein holds itself out for such transformations in its own temporalization of historical and personal life spans. A long forgotten experience can turn out to be of great import to me in what is to come. The French Revolution may come to have a quite different significance in the light of political events to come. Far from requiring us to just wait and see what comes, the moment of vision calls us to act for the sake of a future that gives meaning to what has been and what is, but which itself is never over and done with. The moment of vision calls us to 'take action', although that action can take the form of anything that is possible for Dasein.[27] This may be the moment to remain still, to see something through to the end, to change tack, to backtrack. The moment of vision calls us to make whatever it is we do or do not do an action that gives stretches of time their significance, rather than simply following a chronology, the significance of which has been set out once and for all.

### iii. MEASURING OUT THE DIMENSION

In *Being and Time* Heidegger claims that spatiality must ultimately be understood as grounded in temporality. So the phenomena of spatialization, such as de-severence and orientation, can be interpreted in terms of the ecstases of temporalization.[28] He later radicalizes his understanding of spatiality, arguing that we need to understand temporality and spatiality as originally unified, although fundamentally different facets of the single ongoing event that opens up Dasein's world. In *Contributions to Philosophy (from Enowning)*, for example, Heidegger begins to think in terms of 'time-space'. He unifies his thinking of truth as the opening-preserving of a world of significance with this event that does not take place in time and space but which is time-space. In this event the bringing within reach of spatialization and holding out for what is yet to come of temporalization is rethought as a reciprocal moving towards and removal: 'Time-space as arising from and belonging to the essentialising truth, as the grounded jointure of removal – moving towards (joining) of the there.'[29] The truth of being, understood as an event of opening up that is also a preserving or sheltering, is now thought of as taking place as the removing and moving towards of time-space.

Clearly this is quite different from the representation of space-time in physics as a homogeneous continuum, as Heidegger himself points out.[30] The physicists' representation of space-time is obviously extremely powerful, allowing for a great 'extension of our reach'. Heidegger's concern, however, is quite different. He leads us back to consider how the event of time-space takes place as 'pre-mathematical'. Such a way of thinking about time and space must then give rise to a crucial question: 'How is it that space and time *allow for* mathematization?.'[31] As Heidegger understands it, such a question cannot be answered by presenting us with the calculations and the concepts that arise from those calculations. It can only be addressed by thinking through how time-space takes place as an event that allows for the representation of space and time as calculable dimensions.

All of the multitude of ways of measuring that we pointed out at the beginning of this chapter are kinds of *measuring against*. An object or movement or dimension is taken as the measure for another. So the width of the tree is measured against the reach of my arms. The length of this line is measured against my ruler. In each measuring the measure and/or object of measurement can be exchanged for something else, or even reversed, so that what was being measured is doing the measuring. We could, for example, measure book widths against a ruler or a ruler against book widths. In more formalized measurement, one can measure any dimension against any other. The word 'dimension' itself means that which is measured out. Heidegger does not in the end ask us to abandon measurement, but to consider how anything like a dimension takes place at all prior to the measuring of one object, movement or dimension against another. He concludes that there must be a dimension opened up as 'there' in which every act of measuring one thing against another can take place. *That* measurement cannot be the measurement of one thing against another. It is the original measuring out of a place within which we can measure things against one another. As he puts in his 1951 essay '. . . Poetically Man Dwells . . .': 'Hence it is necessary to pay heed to the basic act of measuring. That consists in man's first of all taking the measure which then is applied to every measuring act.'[32] In measuring out a place for ourselves prior to standards of measurement we 'take the measure' of the dimension within which we can measure one thing against another. Within that dimension all standards of measurement become possible. This dimension is 'prior' but it does not remain open without the acts of measurement by which we stretch out and articulate space and time. In opening a place for itself Dasein creatively opens up a multiplicity of dimensions within that original dimension.

# CHAPTER 8

# WAYS OF LIFE AND DEATH

Life is the beginning of death. Life is for the
sake of death. Death is at once the end and the
beginning – at once separation and closer union
of the self. Through death the reduction is complete.

*Miscellaneous Observations*, 15

Everyone acknowledges that our existence is in some sense finite.
Yet by acknowledging our finitude in this way everyone hopes and
requires that this can be the end of it. We have a tendency to cover
over our finitude even, or especially, by acknowledging it. Everyone
acknowledges that we will all die. There is nothing that is more
readily conceded, nothing more readily acknowledged by one's-self.
This ready acknowledgment is, as is often the case, a way for one to
disguise finitude by levelling it off: 'One *knows* about the certainty
of death, yet "is" not authentically certain of one's own.'[1]

Heidegger was a thinker of finitude. For him, the disclosure of
the world of possibilities could never be completely fulfilled since it
intrinsically involves closure. It is not simply the case that our existence takes place in a stretch of time, but our existence is nothing but
temporalization that stretches out a time for itself. To *be* at all for
anything within the world, to be 'there' somewhere in some sense,
whether discovered or undiscovered, is to be within the finite stretch
of time that Dasein has opened up. The core of Heidegger's own
philosophical motivation was to think through the philosophical
consequences of finitude more radically than it had been thought
before. He hoped to show us that we do not exist as finite within
the infinite, but that discovery of the infinite or experience of
the absolute takes place within finite existence. If we can live as

mortals then we are existing most fully in the finitude that is in any case ours.

## i. THE WHOLE OF LIFE IN DEATH

Heidegger looks towards death, not as a problem concerning the termination of life and what may or may not come after such a termination, but in order to get a better perspective on how Dasein's life is lived. The problem that he sets out to deal with at the beginning of division two of *Being and Time*, having worked through a preliminary investigation of Dasein's 'everydayness' in division one, is how to get Dasein *as a whole* into view.[2] If we recall that Dasein is a being that is interpreting and coming to an understanding of itself, then the reason for its need to grasp itself 'as a whole' becomes apparent. We cannot understand the parts of something properly unless we are able to see how they fit into and form a part of the whole. The problem is that in its 'everyday' dealings Dasein becomes caught up in the involvements of its surrounding world, involvements that do not have an end in themselves, but only in the Dasein itself. One involvement leads on to another. There are breaks in which items become apparent, but they do not limit the whole. In becoming fundamentally attuned to our way of being-in-the-world, as in the experience of anxiety, we experience and begin to understand the whole, but precisely where do we find the 'limit' that makes our lives a whole? Is that something that can be 'brought into view' and if not, how can Dasein experience its existence in the world as a whole?

The problem is not fundamentally with all of the very familiar traits of finitude that belong to the one trying to understand something. For example, we may forget all sorts of particular details belonging to that which we are trying to understand. We may not pick up on details when they are presented to us. If, for example, I am trying to understand a novel, I can read it through and get a sense of the whole without remembering every detail. I may forget large passages and retain a sense of the whole. Of course, my sense of the whole will probably be improved by being reminded of those passages. On the other hand, I may remember the novel in enormous detail. I may even be able to recite large parts of it or even all of it and still have very little or even no sense of the whole. When it comes to understanding ourselves as Dasein we may try to grasp our lives in this manner, as though they were an unfolding plot which we would have to get to the end of in order to understand it as a whole. The fundamental problem facing us might then seem to be the fact that our lives are not yet over. It might seem like trying to understand a novel that we have not yet read to the end. However, Dasein does not finally and completely comprehend itself by coming to its end, but only gains a sense of the whole in the appropriate understanding of its open possibilities. With this as its ontological structure Dasein does not completely understand anything it encounters by finally finishing off that encounter. I can complete a novel, but I do not finally and fully comprehend it upon reading the last sentence, nor at any one point in further interpretative work. Nor is it possible to have every one of its abstract 'possible' meanings spread out before me. I can properly grasp the significance of anything in an open and shared world as being significant *for me*, only when I appropriately grasp my whole ability to understand as limited from within at each moment. This is the way of being that Heidegger calls 'being-towards-death.'

If Dasein is a continuing opening up and negotiation of its own world, if it is coming to an understanding and interpretation of itself, then how can it get a view of the whole when it is still continuing into what is yet to come?

The problem seems to exist so long as Dasein exists, because Dasein is always an ability to be that is projected into the future, suggesting that, since it is those possibilities, it is *not yet* itself: 'An entity whose essence is made up of existence, is essentially opposed to the possibility of our getting it in our grasp as an entity which is a whole.'[3] The problem is not one of trying to determine 'how I will die,' what will happen at the end of life, or anything of that nature. Rather, we are faced with the problem of understanding anything at all of life, if we are the kind of being that resists being grasped as a whole, if we hold ourselves out into the future that is yet to come. To understand ourselves we need to grasp the whole, but we cannot do this in the manner of having every possible meaning of every affect, action and word, present and in our possession. Nevertheless, death gives us the possibility of grasping the whole of our Dasein in another way, because it is a singular limit in each case, a limit that is already there for Dasein, rather than as an occurrence that will come about at one stage or another and 'wrap up' life more or less adequately.

Death as Heidegger thinks of it is not what happens at the opposite end of life from birth. What takes place at the end of life he names 'demise.'[4] Dasein's demise is never simply coming to an end or 'perishing,' because it has the ontological structure of being-with others. So even if it is alone in death and lies undiscovered, even if all trace of it has apparently been lost, it may always be recovered as significant for another. In the potentiality that another Dasein has for making it and its demise a part of its life, even after its demise, Dasein has not simply come to an end. Death, on the other hand, is neither simply coming to an end nor demising: 'Death in the widest sense is a phenomenon of life.'[5] Put simply, we are dying from the start, whether we realize it or not. Heidegger cites a passage from Johannes von Tepl's poem *Ploughman of Bohemia*: 'As soon as man comes to life, he is at once old enough to die.'[6] Or as we find it in the more mischievous expression of Samuel Beckett: 'Birth was the death of him.'[7] We are born into death, not as the particular demise that will come at the end, but as a possibility that is already there, giving every other possibility its character. Death is not one possibility amongst others, but the singular possibility that makes all of my possibilities singularly mine. There is just my death that I must face, indeterminate but mine whatever it may be. Death is already there for Dasein as the limit of all its possibilities, internal to every possibility: 'Dasein, as thrown being-in-the-world, has in every case already been delivered over to its death. In being towards its death, Dasein is dying factically and indeed constantly, so long as it has not yet come to its demise.'[8] Death does not then become some external motivational force, pushing us to choose because 'time is running out.' Death may cut off the fulfillment of any choice, even if made in good time. Neither does 'being-towards-death' allow Dasein to securely calculate which choices it should make. Being-towards-death gives Dasein the potential to take up or let go of each of its possibilities as belonging to its singular and whole ability to be in the world.

Heidegger addresses two initial misunderstandings of the thought that Dasein can grasp itself as a whole in being-towards-death. Being-towards-death cannot signify any special propensity towards the termination of life. It cannot require Dasein to endanger its life or bring its life to an end. Once Dasein is no more, then that is the end of all its abilities. Termination is the termination of all understanding.[9] So Dasein will not acquire the ability to grasp itself as a whole through its own termination. That is not to say that in living out its possibilities and choices a Dasein may not be faced with termination and even resolutely choose termination. The essential point is that Dasein does not grasp itself as a whole and face its possibilities as its own *because* it risks its life or brings about its own demise. Rather, it is because it is faced with its own death that there is a difference for it between simply walking into such possibilities and understanding their significance for this very Dasein that it is.

Another apparent solution to the problem of grasping Dasein as a whole is to look towards the lives and deaths of others. Since we can still be there when others cease to be and there are many others who are already dead, if we want to understand Dasein as a whole, do we not simply need to turn towards lives that have already come to an end? There are a number of reasons why this move cannot provide us with a solution. Although after death another is no longer there and has lost every ability to understand, this does not mean that the actions and events that made up that life have ceased to take on significance in the light of what takes place for those who are still there after that death. As Heidegger points out, our concern for the dead in funeral and burial rites is premised upon the fact that this being is 'still more' than equipment to be made use of or a bare physical object.[10] One can, for example, be dishonoured in death and this can reflect upon how that which occurred during one's life is understood by those who are still there. We might have thought that looking towards the lives of those who are dead would give us a sealed and finally complete comprehension of them, but that is not the case. Often we only begin to understand others after their demise. We are looking for the wrong kind of delimitation for a being that is or has been there in the manner of Dasein. It is only when Dasein's own life is delimited in an appropriate way that it can begin to properly engage with and understand the lives of others who are there with it, together with those who have been there and ultimately those who will be there and are already there for us.

Dasein has a deep tendency to try to understand itself in terms which are not appropriate to its way of being and which prevent it from grasping itself as a whole. The various inappropriate ways of viewing death derive from trying to grasp it as a kind of end or limit that belongs to something present-at-hand or ready-to-hand within the world. Some beings seem to have a character of 'not yet' comparable to Dasein's being its possibilities, but this can be quite misleading. Heidegger examines various analogies of this kind, some of which are more helpful than others. When it is in its last quarter the moon is 'not yet' full, but in that case the moon is already complete and actual; it is simply not perceived as full in its present phase.[11] Dasein, on the other hand, *is* its possibilities which are not yet actual. Closer to Dasein's way of being is a ripening fruit, because it has ripeness as the possibility that makes it what it is, even when it is not yet ripe. However, whilst death is the possibility that makes us who we are even when it has not yet come about, it is unlike ripeness, because the fruit is 'fulfilled' when it is ripe, whilst Dasein is no longer there when death arrives. At the end Dasein is not most fully itself, but no longer itself at all, even though it was this possibility of death that delimited it all along.[12] A number of other comparisons also turn out to be inadequate. Dasein does not 'stop' in the sense that a rain shower stops or a road stops. In the former case 'stopping' means being no longer present-at-hand, whilst in the latter it means being present as this particular road because it ends here. Neither captures that character of Dasein's limitation, which is already there, but never present or actual. Nor does Dasein get 'finished' like a particular work, such as a painting, or like equipment that can get used up, like bread that gets finished off.[13] In any such comparison Dasein is identified with a determinate actuality or determinate set of possibilities, such determination being the delimitation of items or equipment within the world. But the delimitation of Dasein is precisely opposed to this. Dasein is limited, and as such 'defined' and delimited in its own way as a singular whole in each case, *because* its possibilities cannot be fixed and determined in this way, since they are all potentially nothing in the face of death.

The existential conception of death that Heidegger develops shows death to possess a number of crucial characteristics that clarify the internal delimitation that Dasein's finitude gives its possibilities. What makes death Dasein's 'ownmost possibility,' is that it is non-relational, not to be outstripped and certain. Firstly, death is not like any of Dasein's other possibilities because it is non-relational, which is to say that it is not a possibility that we can take over from or for others. Thus Heidegger claims that: '*No one can take the other's dying away from him.*'[14] There is no stepping in for or representing another in death. One can, of course, 'step in' for another in the face of a particular risk. I can take a bullet for another and so forth, but that will at most save the other from a particular demise, not from death. Furthermore, although it is not a consequence of this non-relationality that I will necessarily feel isolated as I come to the end, dying is what I must do myself and indeed, it is because Dasein dies that it is individualized. The non-relationality that belongs to death actually means that Dasein can have a singular kind of relationship with others, namely, one in which there is no question of someone else 'stepping in' for this singular Dasein or replacing him or her: 'As the non-relational possibility, death individualizes – but only in such a manner that, as the possibility that is not to be outstripped, it makes Dasein, as being-with, have some understanding of the ability-to-be of others.'[15] Individualized in the face of death, Dasein can understand the individuality and singularity of others.

Death is 'not to be outstripped,' that is, Dasein cannot get around it or escape it, even though it may be able to avoid some particular end. Importantly, this is also the case for Dasein in its everyday being as it seeks to avoid facing death as its ownmost possibility, attempting to externalize it with the claim that: 'Death certainly comes, but not right away.'[16] The numerous tactics employed by the everyday 'one's-self' to try to evade death are all actually ways in which Dasein can be towards this very possibility, even as it attempts to make itself indifferent to it.[17] Dasein 'falls' into the world, attempting to evade or get around death, but in doing so it acknowledges escape to be impossible. Here we also find Dasein mistaking the character of death's certainty, which should not be taken as being of the same order as knowledge, even knowledge of the highest probability. Death is certain as that which can come at any moment, potentially cutting off all of Dasein's possibilities.[18] To *be* certain of this is not to be in possession of a particular item of knowledge, which may or may not be understood in connection to other items of knowledge. Dasein can *be* certain of death, in the way that it lives out its possibilities, even without ever formulating a proposition of the kind, 'Everyone must die.' Formulating such a proposition and trying to assess its validity is an externalization and generalization of *my own* death as the kind of thing that belongs to everyone. I can be certain of death even without ever considering that particular occurrence that will bring about my demise. To be certain of death is to live out all of my possibilities as characterized by this internal delimitation; at any moment they can come to nothing.

In the end there is no comprehensive solution to the problem constantly posed by Dasein to itself, namely, how to understand itself when all its possibilities of understanding project it ahead of itself. Grasping itself 'as a whole' cannot mean to get a comprehensive overview of all that it is capable and incapable of. If it tries to fully comprehend itself in this way, it fails to understand itself appropriately. Nevertheless, Dasein is capable in each case, whatever its abilities may be, of being those abilities in a way open to the indeterminate and constant threat of being brought to nothing. It is because Dasein opens the world through each and every one of its capabilities, that its being-in-the-world can be closed at any moment and brought to nothing by death. By opening itself to this incapacity that will never be got around, no matter what it brings within its power, Dasein is capable of being its own 'authentic' self. Yet because this *inability* is an inescapable characteristic of all of its abilities, it will never fully take possession of itself once and for all. It is itself in everything that it can be, as a whole, a being that faces its incapacity to fully actualize or finally comprehend everything that it can be.

## ii. A CALL TO INSECURE FREEDOM

What, if anything, are we supposed to learn from all of this? Is there a lesson to be learnt from our finitude about how we are to live our finite lives? In an important sense there is no lesson at all and nothing to be learnt. These reflections are not supposed to tell us what sort of things we should be doing: 'it is not as if norms and rules for comporting oneself towards death were to be proposed for "edification".'[19] The problem of being towards death is the problem that we all face in being alive. It is the problem of how to live lives that make sense by negotiating a field of possibility, when we do not have a complete life, or even a number of abstract and disconnected 'possible' lives, available or present before us. Far from trying to take this problem away from us, to solve it for us by proposing a set of norms and rules for living, Heidegger is trying to give this problem back to us. Our deepest tendency is to try to abdicate from facing the problem. Such abdication does not relieve us of the problem as we hope it will, since whatever we choose will still be a response to the problem. Yet in responding we usually refuse to understand the necessity of taking up some possibilities and not others as problematic. In taking up the problem for ourselves, on the other hand, we are freed for our own possibilities. In this way we find *freedom towards death*.[20] That freedom comes with the recognition that our being always ahead of ourselves, makes every choice we make inherently *insecure*. Our choices may not come to mean what we think, hope, desire or will them to mean. They may indeed come to nothing. Rather than living under the illusion that we can find a final set of rules and regulations which, if absorbed and observed will make us free, this freedom comes precisely in the recognition that the taking up of any possibilities is inherently insecure, because it is made on the basis of what is not yet. In being-toward-death we do not find any completely secure path, but we take up the problem of negotiating a path that cannot be fully secured.

There are several important phenomena that Heidegger analyzes in *Being and Time* in connection with the difficulty of trying to give ourselves back the problem of our own lives. The first is what he terms the 'call of conscience.' This phenomenon is easily confused with what for Heidegger is its complete antithesis: a voice that tells us 'do this' or 'do not do that.' Conscience calls us, Heidegger argues, not primarily to do this or not to do that, but it calls us back to ourselves. This makes it a very peculiar phenomenon. It is a call from 'nobody.' Conscience comes not from a particular person, nor group of persons, nor from a super-natural personality.[21] Yet it is not the anonymous claim of the 'nobody in particular' of the One. What does the call say? It does not tell us to do this or that, to live in this way or that way. Strictly speaking, it says nothing![22] The call is a silent appeal, from Dasein to itself, calling it back to itself.[23] Of course, so far as the One is concerned, a call from nobody that tells us nothing is itself nothing at all. It means nothing and does not exist. The only call that One recognizes could be recognized by anyone, as a call that offers advice and criteria by which one can judge right and wrong, correct or incorrect. The call of conscience offers none of that and so is nothing at all so far as everyone is concerned. Yet it is only in response to the call that we cease to abdicate our own freedom, because the call calls us to recognize the always problematic and insecure nature of any criteria of choice. When we respond to the call we cannot be said to 'have a conscience,' as some secure possession, but we are put in the position of 'wanting to have a conscience.'[24] The greatest abdication of freedom and failure to respond to the call of conscience comes when we are satisfied that we have a 'good conscience.' If we try to escape responsibility by sharply delineating what we are and are not responsible for, living and acting in a shared and open world means that securing a good conscience would ultimately involve abdicating all responsibility. When we cease wanting to have a conscience and start to think of ourselves as in possession of a good conscience, we stop responding to the call of conscience.

That Dasein is called to continually respond to the call of conscience by wanting to have a conscience indicates that Dasein cannot get around its own finitude. It has a certain 'not' character, or 'notness.'[25] The finitude of Dasein, its 'not-character' amounts to this, that by existing Dasein discloses this world for itself, laying the basis for its own existence, and yet it can never have this basis fully within its power.[26] Why not? As a temporalizing disclosure of the world, Dasein is always oriented towards a future which is 'not yet' and potentially nothing. We are orientated towards the future, but we plainly never have it in our grasp. As we move into that future we take up some possibilities and in doing so necessarily let others fall away. Freedom is the choice of possibilities and the falling away of others: 'Freedom, however, *is* only in the choice of *one* possibility – that is, in tolerating one's not having chosen the others and in one's not being able to choose them.'[27] We should thus not think of our finitude as the lack of something that would ideally be present. We have possibilities and abilities precisely because we *cannot* choose everything. If we had the basis of our own existence fully within our power, if we did not have to choose possibilities and let others fall away, if we did not have this 'not-character' as our way of being, this would not make us freer, it would make us incapable of freedom. To be capable of freedom is to be capable in our *incapacity* to do it all.

Thus we encounter a second phenomenon in this ongoing struggle to free ourselves for our own possibilities, that of 'being-guilty.' What Heidegger has in mind when he writes of this existential character of being-guilty is again easily misunderstood. Above all, it does not indicate that Dasein has a particular propensity to do bad and evil things. Rather, it is simply because we are finite and that in doing one thing we cannot do others that we are guilty.

As Heidegger puts it in a lecture just prior to *Being and Time*: 'Every action is at the same time something marked by guilt. For the possibilities of action are limited in comparison with the demands of conscience, so that every action that is successfully carried out produces conflicts. Insofar as I am at all, I become guilty whenever I act in any sense.'[28] We can be morally responsible or become morally culpable because we are free and are thus necessarily guilty in this sense.[29] This is not a call to evil nor to complacency in the light of some purported idea that evil is unavoidable. It is a call to realize our finite freedom and as such a call away from all complacency.

Does it follow that 'being-guilty' involves an oppressive moral assessment of ourselves as never being good enough? Friedrich Nietzsche had argued that this is precisely what the moral and religious concepts of guilt entail. Has Heidegger not just reworked that concept to make it, if anything, even more deeply rooted, so that we are now guilty simply by virtue of being and doing anything at all? Nietzsche had argued in the second of his three essays *On the Genealogy of Morality* that our current concepts of religious and moral guilt are really only perversions of political, legal, material and economic indebtedness, making this connection through the German word '*Schuld*,' which means both guilt and debt. We think of moral guilt as a kind of debt which we owe but can never pay back. God has given us life and we owe everything to Him. Christianity then puts a peculiar twist on this logic, having Jesus make the once and for all final payment on our behalf, since we could never pay it ourselves. In his sacrifice we bizarrely find 'God paying himself back.'[30] Heidegger agrees with Nietzsche that a great deal of our moral thinking and commonsense understanding of our own condition is conducted in terms of this economic analogy. Yet whilst Nietzsche hopes to free us from the debt of moral guilt that only God can write off for us by tracing its origin back to much more manageable legal and material debts, Heidegger does not think this goes far enough. We then still think of Dasein as a household whose income needs to be balanced with its payments: 'a way of interpreting which forces Dasein's existence to be subsumed under the idea of a business procedure that can be regulated.'[31] The real problem is that we think of Dasein in terms of some kind of economic transaction at all. Nietzsche might free us from a particularly perverted way of understanding that transaction, but in doing so he seems to reinforce the understanding of 'guilt' or 'indebtedness,' as something to be paid back and thus a certain relation to our future as regular and calculable. For Heidegger, Dasein's being as a finite being makes it 'guilty' in the sense of not being able to do everything and 'indebted' in the sense of not having this basis for all of its abilities completely in its grasp. It is this that makes it possible that Dasein should become morally guilty or indebted to others. Yet whilst becoming morally guilty or materially indebted are both possibilities for us because we are finite, they are possibilities that we free ourselves for, not in having everything in control in advance and thus being able to calculate precisely what is coming, but possibilities which we are only *free* for because we cannot entirely secure the future. It is 'being-guilty' in Heidegger's ontological sense that allows us to be open to the future in a way that we can take on debt or responsibility without ever being able to fully secure that future. Such freedom that cannot secure everything in advance might, amongst its possibilities, allow for the undermining of a morally secure world that makes us all unworthy sinners in advance or of a socio-economic world that makes the majority into hopeless debtors in advance.

Once more, Heidegger does not want to tell us what we should do in response to our finitude, but shows us how it is that we can respond freely. Since Dasein exists by projecting open a future which it does not have fully in its power, its possibilities are never laid out before it in a complete system. What it is able to do is to exist in *anticipation* of its future. Anticipation is clearly not knowledge of the future, but the taking up of the amorphous and indeterminate set of possibilities that our situation presents us with and making them into a choice to be made. To do that we must anticipate what is to come. Anticipation is reciprocally connected at root with the commitments of resolute disclosure that we discussed in Chapter 6. It is only through anticipation of what is to come that we can try to make our commitments appropriate and only through resolute commitment that we can anticipate what is to come, rather than simply waiting to see what comes along. This is how Dasein can become authentically itself, but none of this frees it from finitude. Rather, it is freed for its own finitude, that is, freed to take up some possibilities that it discloses for itself and to let others fall away. Anticipatory resoluteness, by which we freely respond to ourselves as a whole even though we cannot *know* what is to come, is anything but a rigid sticking to principles come what may. What is disclosed to us in our resolution may require a fundamental response and change of commitment: 'The certainty of resolution signifies that one *holds oneself free for* the possibility of *taking it back* [. . .]'[32] Anticipatory resoluteness requires us to participate more fully in the negotiation that discloses the world as incomplete, a negotiation through which alone our resolutions may be justified, but never fully secured.

### iii. PHILOSOPHY SACRALIZED

It is easy to detect a religious motivation behind Heidegger's thought, especially when it involves, as it does in *Being and Time*, a reworking of conscience and guilt as ontologically grounded in Dasein's very way of being. This has led many to suspect that what Heidegger is trying to provide us with is some kind of secularized theology.[33] Whether or not such an assessment is appropriate, of course, depends upon what is meant by secularization and that in turn depends upon an understanding of what is it is to be religious. Heidegger had a 'religious' background, in the Catholic faith and in the study of theology. In the early 1920s he also engaged in an extended study of Luther's theological writings that had a significant influence on him.[34] He moved away from doctrinal positions, but he was clearly exercised by the question of what religious faith is and what theology may or may not involve. At the same time he maintained from the start that philosophy has as its calling not the maintenance and upholding of positions and doctrines, but ever renewed appropriate questioning that does not rest on its laurels. As he says in 1953, 'questioning is the piety of thought.'[35] If secularized theology means anything like an attempt to make those without faith swallow theological dogma, then there is nothing of that kind in Heidegger's thought. If it means that theological concepts are interpreted in a secular age that no longer takes the being of eternity as its starting point, then Heidegger did think that philosophy and perhaps theology can undertake such a task.[36] What he was concerned with above all, however, is that we should not simply recycle the concepts that have been used by any Dasein in coming to an understanding of itself, but re-activate them in our own way of coming to understand ourselves.

From early on Heidegger is less interested in the speculative doctrines that particular religious institutions uphold as in the thinking through of what it means to live a religious life. When thinking of the 'primal' Christian life, for example, he describes a life that is trying to work out for itself what its religiosity consists in. This is something that can still be found in later Christianity but it tends to be covered over by doctrinal institutionalization. What we need to do is to *reactivate* the self-questioning interpretation of the religious life in order to understand the motivation behind the doctrines. Such a reactivation is the aim of his own interpretations of early Christian life, such as the readings of letters from St Paul that he undertook in lectures from 1920–21: 'The dogma as detached content of doctrine in an objective, epistemological emphasis could never have been guiding for Christian religiosity. On the contrary, the genesis of dogma can only be understood from out of the enactment of Christian life experience.'[37] By 1927 Heidegger concludes that if we are to think of religious life as a particular kind of life trying to understand itself, then we need to base our interpretation of that life on a thoroughgoing interrogation of self-interpretation itself, that is, a 'fundamental ontology' of Dasein. Faith as a way of life, a 'reborn' life, is still grounded in the pre-faithful existential life of Dasein, of which faith is a specific existentiell elaboration. Thus, 'All theological concepts necessarily contain *that* understanding of being that is constitutive of human Dasein as such, insofar as it exists at all.'[38] Theological concepts can contain philosophical formal indications, but philosophy is not bound to those particular indications. That is not to say that philosophy will have nothing to say about the religious life, but what it does have to say will be said with regard to its being a mode of Dasein's life rather than specifically directed towards its religiosity. Theology is significant insofar as it contains and leads one towards philosophy, but philosophy itself is not bound to theology or the life of faith.

Nevertheless, philosophical thought has been bound to theology more deeply than is usually suspected. This is not just a matter of many important philosophers having led religious lives and introducing theological concerns and concepts into their philosophical thinking. Nor is it something that is simply undone by the fact that many people now think that philosophy should be divorced from theology understood as dogmatic adherence to creeds. In his later thought, right up until some of his final writings, Heidegger understood the whole of Western metaphysics as being what he calls onto-theology.[39] Every inquiry into what it means for something to be 'ontology,' has been essentially accompanied by a thinking of what has the *most being*, or better, what it is that underwrites and secures the being of everything, 'theology.'[40] That which underwrites the being of beings, the *theos*, is not necessarily understood as a personal omnipotent and benevolent supernatural being. A great many metaphysicians, from Aristotle to Spinoza and beyond, have denied that there is any such being. Nevertheless, their thought is onto-theological because their understanding of what it means for something to be is essentially connected to an understanding of that which underwrites or grounds being. The most hard-nosed logically and scientifically minded philosophers today, however much they may disparage phrases such as 'the ground of being,' are very often quite clearly engaged in onto-theology. Whenever logical coherence is invoked as a criterion for deciding what can and cannot be, we are engaged in thinking about the grounds of being. Or if, for example, the mathematical structure worked out in the natural sciences is understood as telling us what *really* exists and underwrites the existence of everything else, we are engaged in a thinking of the grounds of being.

We are so deeply immersed in this metaphysical tradition of onto-theology that it would be impossible for us to simply lay it to one side. Yet at the root of Heidegger's philosophizing is an experience of the radical finitude of the sense or truth of being and thus of the grounding of being. Dasein must underwrite its own existence and with that the being of everything that appears within its world, that is, beings as a whole. Yet there is nothing that underwrites and secures that laying of the ground for metaphysics, nothing that guarantees the ground we lay for ourselves. So the ground of being is grounded in an 'abyss' or withdrawal of ground.[41] The thinking that recognizes that finitude, extending even to the ground of being, is not necessarily cut off from any experience of the divine, the sacred or the holy. But it cannot make the divine into the ground that underwrites its own questioning and interpretation as it grounds thought and being. Such an experience of the divine would no longer serve as an absolute guarantee but will be the refusal of all absolute guarantees. The experience of the divine, if it does come, will come as a participant in the finite opening of an always incomplete world, not as the absolute guarantor of a world finally fulfilled.

# CHAPTER 9

# ORIGIN AND ORIGINALITY

The history of philosophy up to now is nothing but a history of attempts to discover how to do philosophy. As soon as we do philosophy – philosophemes come into being, and the true natural history of philosophemes is *philosophy*.

*Logological Fragments* I, 1

We have inherited a misguided understanding of the relation of history to philosophical thinking. Our view of the place of history in philosophy stems from a misguided view of the place of history in Dasein's existence. History is not simply background knowledge that may allow us to avoid falling into the errors of the past. There is no getting the history out of the way to start afresh. Whatever we attempt, whether it be philosophical thought or anything else, history is not at bottom some special interest which we can choose to pursue or not; it is an unavoidable aspect of Dasein's temporalizing existence. To start afresh can only be to start afresh with history, which means not just what has happened, but how it is that we are open to what has happened. Historical science itself is a particular way in which Dasein can 'historicize' time. As such, it has its condition of possibility in the historicizing of Dasein, the openness to what has been that stretches itself along. Heidegger marks this distinction by calling the historizing of time that belongs to Dasein as such its 'historicality' (*Geschichtlichkeit*), while that way of historizing that is orientated towards knowing the past 'historiology' (*Historie*).[1] We can develop a science of the past only because we exist historically and are open to the past.[2] However, we cannot simply rely upon established procedures to give us access to the past, because those procedures themselves will have to be historically inherited.

In our historical existence we always belong to tradition. In inheriting the past we tend to make that tradition as we receive it into 'the' tradition. Yet if we actually engage with that tradition it will quickly become apparent that 'the' tradition is never self-identical, precisely because it only becomes tradition in the way it is inherited. In philosophizing, as in anything else, we belong to tradition and we understand ourselves in terms of tradition. We are also constantly setting ourselves apart from tradition, taking traditions forward and even revolutionizing them, but in doing so we still belong to them. Philosophizing is the thoughtful engagement with a tradition of thought that tries to understand how that engagement can take place. At the beginning of the philosophical tradition, 'traditionally' designated as Presocratic Greek philosophizing, this was already what was taking place, in a thoughtful engagement with what was already thought in the religious, mythological, mathematical and proto-scientific traditions. Thinking cannot be an 'eternal' a-historical conversation about timeless concerns. But that does not mean that what is thought can only concern those who live in a particular period. As temporalizing and historizing beings we are still coming to an understanding of ourselves by continuing to come to terms with where we have come from.

## i. ORIGINAL DESTRUCTION

To recover what is original in thinking we need to engage in destruction. Heidegger calls for nothing less that the destruction of the whole ontological tradition.[3] This is not only the task he set himself, but the task, he claims, of any philosophizing that wants to think originally. What is accomplished in destruction is not a preliminary to original thought; it is thought trying to think through what was originally being thought. Destruction does not have a negative aim, since it does not seek to annihilate or obliterate the tradition. Destruction does not need to be balanced by positive constructive thinking; it is itself positive and constructive thinking. What it aims to achieve is the recovery of 'those primordial experiences in which we achieved our first ways of determining the nature of being.'[4] It cannot do that by laying the tradition to one side or trying to obliterate it, but only by positively engaging with it.

There is, nevertheless, a certain negativity in this positive engagement. It comes not from trying to obliterate the past, nor from trying to show where past thinkers went wrong or made mistakes. The negativity of the positive engagement that Heidegger calls destruction comes from trying to think through to the limits of the 'primordial experiences' of the nature of being. That means, trying to place that thought within its original horizon and world of intelligibility and in so doing thinking about what could not be intelligible in that horizon. In doing so it is not as though we could avoid thinking within a horizon of possible significance that we have opened up for ourselves. Therefore, we also need to try to carry out a destruction of our own understanding of what has been thought. In fact, trying to think about the horizon of what is intelligible to us, our world of possible significance, is precisely what is positive in philosophical thought. The real mistake in philosophical research is to separate the negative and the positive. As Heidegger puts it when undertaking one of his first destructive recoveries of Aristotle's ontology: 'Just as there is destruction in phenomenological research, so too, unified with the destruction, there is phenomenological-existentiell composition.'[5] That is to say, in trying to break up all received understandings of concepts that point towards an horizon of significance from which they arose, Dasein is at the same time constructing or projecting an horizon of significance within which to understand them.

This is a quite different understanding of originality from the one that is generally received. Descartes is for many the paradigm case of originality in philosophical thought. The tradition to which we belong has made self-evident a conception of originality that is derived from Descartes' understanding of how philosophical thought must begin. The self-evidence of this concept of originality almost certainly does not do justice to Descartes' own understanding of the relationship of his thought to that of his predecessors, but this is precisely Heidegger's point. We become enthralled to a tradition that becomes so self-evident that we feel no need to recover its origins. The conception of originality that has become self-evident contends that we must first lay aside all thoughts and opinions that have been handed down to us from tradition and inculcated in us by our experiences and education and then start from scratch. As Descartes put it in the first of his *Meditations on First Philosophy*, what he wanted to do was, 'demolish everything completely and start again right from the foundations'.[6] This was to be achieved by employing a rigorous method of doubt. We are to set aside everything that can possibly be doubted until we reach a point at which doubt is not possible and this is the foundation upon which we can build. What cannot be doubted, for Descartes, is that he is a thinking being and as such exists, since by doubting he confirms this. Philosophical method is thus divided into its positive and negative moments. One destroys in order to rebuild more solidly. However, as more than one reader of Descartes has noticed, that rebuilding actually seems to rely on a great many concepts and arguments that are not wholly new, but can be found in the scholastic tradition which Descartes was educated into. Neither is it the case that he simply used some of the same terminology. Rather, Heidegger argues that through a 'destructive' reading of Descartes we can see a profound sense in which he occupied the same horizon of intelligibility as that opened up by medieval and ultimately ancient ontology.[7] None of this is to detract from Descartes' originality. His thought initiated a decisive shift in what is intelligible to us and opened up new possibilities of significance. The point is that if we want to recover what was original in that thought and to think originally ourselves, we need to engage destructively with it in such a way that we draw out the horizon of possible meaning within which it makes sense to think in that way.

Heidegger's view of the essential and unavoidable historicality of philosophical thought, rooted in the historicality of Dasein, leads him to some unusual conclusions about what philosophizing involves and how it should be undertaken. The negative moment and the positive moment are united in the destructive recovery of the original source of philosophical concepts. That original source is the way that a particular Dasein, always along with others, lived out the existential possibilities of existence for itself. Thinking and determining that origin can only involve another Dasein living out its own possibilities for recovering what has been, including what has been thought. So it is not a question of knocking down and then building up again. The traditional distinction between historical and systematic philosophy becomes highly problematic. In the usual account everything is geared towards producing one's own distinctive systematic treatment of the issue at hand. Historical research is a propaedeutic to the production of this systematic account, allowing us to survey the ways in which a problem has been tackled in the past so as to see what we can take from the past, what can be salvaged, so we can leave the rest behind. Heidegger understood things quite differently. What we are aiming at in phenomenological research is to move through how things usually appear in 'everyday' understanding, to the world of possible meaning or horizon of intelligibility that allows us to understand in that way and then finally to think about *how* that horizon comes about. This field of research is 'historiological in its innermost grounds' and precedes the partition of philosophical knowledge into systematic and historical.[8] In the lecture course *The Basic Problems of Phenomenology*, Heidegger identifies three 'components', or aspects, of phenomenological research as reduction, construction and destruction.[9] Reduction takes us from beings to an understanding of their being (i.e., the horizon of intelligibility) and finally to the question of what it means to be (i.e., how that horizon comes about). Construction is bringing ourselves forwards in a positive projection of being, which is to say, this research can only be undertaken within the horizon of intelligibility that we are bringing about. We must at the same time engage in a destruction of our own 'understanding of being' or horizon of intelligibility, if we are not simply to take our own world for granted, but to think through how it has come about: 'Construction in philosophy is necessarily destruction (*Destruktion*), that is to say, a de-constructing (*Abbau*) of traditional concepts carried out in a historical recursion to the tradition.'[10] Destruction or deconstruction requires us to recover the original horizon of intelligibility within which concepts that have become self-evident were developed. However, that is carried out through a constructive projection of our own horizon of intelligibility.

The result is that there is no single unique locus of an original thought process, but originality is only to be recovered in a constructive engagement with a complex tradition that is always in danger of falling once more into self-evidence. Heidegger thus developed a conception of original thinking that has become almost unintelligible for us insofar as we simply inherit the idea of originality as a complete break from the past:

> Originality consists in nothing other than decisively seeing and thinking once again at the right moment of vision that which is essential, that which has already been repeatedly seen and

thought before. Human history is such that it ensures that what is seen again in this way gets buried once again in time.[11]

## ii. HISTORY REPEATS ITSELF

Since philosophy cannot avoid the historicality of existence any more than any other thought and action that Dasein undertakes, it becomes a central task for philosophy as Heidegger understands it to come to terms with that historicality. How is it that the past comes down to us? On the one hand, the past penetrates every aspect of our existence, including our most abstract and apparently timeless thoughts. The past is given to us and makes us who we are, whether we like it or not and whether we know it or not. Usually what comes to us from the past is taken to be self-evident. On the other hand, even when it is taken in this way, what comes to us from the past must be *taken up* into our own world as self-evident. Dasein is taking up its own past. Even when we do not realize that our thoughts and actions come to us from the past, we have taken up and appropriated that origin into our own world. What has been is *taken* for granted by everyday existence, but that means that we must be taking it up and understanding what it has left to us, even when we are unaware of what we are doing. That is why Heidegger claims that Dasein has an historical existence, even when it is not aware of its past, let alone whether or not it has knowledge gleaned from historical sciences. The task for destructive historical philosophizing becomes one of relating to and taking up its own past in such a way that the past together with our way of taking it up is no longer taken for granted. It is an attempt to take up the past in an explicit *repetition*.

Repetition allows us to take up the past as our own and thus to become 'authentically' historical.[12] Historicality, after all, is not simply the fact that certain things took place in the past. Historicality is the past brought into Dasein's world and relived, and it is only as such that the past can 'influence' what is now taking place and what is yet to come. Since Dasein always understands its present in terms of the possibilities that are yet to come for it, the past that we repeat in our present is understood in terms of our future. The result is that history is not primarily a matter of the past, or rather, insofar as it is a matter of the past it is the past not as that which is now over and done with, but as that which is occurring again and is still to occur for us. Repetition does not take us back into the past or tie the present to the past in such a way that we cut off what is potentially new: 'Rather, the repetition makes a *reciprocative rejoinder* to the possibility of that existence which has-been-there.'[13] That is, the past can speak to us, but only if we learn how to ask about it and then allow what we find to modify our way of understanding and asking. We often suppose that our relationship to the past is one-sided. Either we suppose the past to be transparent, simply yielding to us what it has to say, or it is thought to be utterly opaque, such that anything it says to us will be a question of what we make it say. However, our encounter with the past, as with all of Dasein's encounters, is a matter of reciprocal negotiation. We will not be able to think through what the past means to us if we simply accept it in the terms in which it has been received, but neither can we think it through if we simply impose our own terms upon it. The terms of the past make no sense if we do not make them our own, while our own terms will in one way or another be taken from the past in any case. The past speaks in answer to the questions that we pose to it, but those questions themselves are in part a response to what the past has handed down to us.

What exactly does repetition involve? Heidegger's term 'repetition' (*Wiederholung*), is also sometimes translated as 'retrieval', both terms having the sense of collecting, gathering or fetching something again. Repetition does not here have the sense of precisely the same happening again. Heidegger's understanding of the on-going contextual involvement of things and occurrences in the world means that 'the same again' can only mean something taken from its context. Yet repetition does not mean taking some occurrence, action or thought out of its 'original context' and transplanting it into a 'new context', i.e. our own context. That way of thinking about what takes place assumes that the 'context' is something that is set up in some way independently from what happens for Dasein, including what it does or what it thinks. This is to give the 'world' the character of a complex of things that contains these occurrences, deeds and thoughts. But the world as 'context' does not have that character; it is an horizon of what can be understood by Dasein as it is in the world, feeling, understanding and speaking. Thus we can call the context, following one of Heidegger's early formulations, a 'complex of enactment'. The context is not just a set of detachable surroundings to an action or thought, but rather: 'The complex of enactment determines itself in and with the enactment.'[14] Historical repetition is thus a kind of 're-enactment', but not one that is the same thing again transplanted into a new context. Rather, it takes up what the enactment of the situational complex is and enacts it again as part of the bringing about of our own world of significance.

If repetition does not 'bring again' what is past and does not involve abandoning itself to the past,[15] if it is a re-enactive engagement with the past, does that mean that we can simply repeat at will without constraint, making the past say whatever we want it to say? Clearly the past is not simply open to us to make of it what we will any more than any other aspect of our self-interpretative thought and action. We present ourselves with certain possibilities which we cannot simply get around or manipulate at will. This situation is reflected in our historicality in two ways. Firstly, what we repeat is not just 'what really happened'. The nineteenth century German historian Leopold von Ranke famously claimed that the business of history is not to moralize but to find out 'wie es eigentlich gewesen ist', which is frequently translated as 'what actually happened'.[16] Finding out what actually happened is not an easy task, but it is not the full extent of our task when we engage with the past. If it were we would not actually be able to fulfill that task properly, because we would not understand what it meant for what actually happened to happen. What we need to repeat is not just what actually happened, but the situational world of possibilities within which it happened. We need to repeat the horizon of possibilities that did not happen, possibilities that give what did actually happen its sense: '*Repetition is handing down explicitly* – that is to say, going back into the possibility of the Dasein that has-been-there.'[17] On this understanding of our relation to the past, we might re-translate Ranke's aphorism regarding the task that faces us in re-enacting the past as finding out 'how it actually has been' for Dasein faced with its own possibilities.

Secondly, the fact that Dasein presents itself with possibilities that it cannot simply manipulate at will reflects back upon its repetition of the past because repetition itself has its possibilities that are not timeless, but historically informed. The possibilities that we have available to us for repeating the past are part of the dispensation of the historical tradition to which we belong. Repetition of the tradition occurs in many ways which do not directly involve historical sciences and the knowledge they produce. Dasein belongs to a tradition and is able to repeat its past whether or not those sciences are a possibility for it. Indeed, historiology itself includes many possibilities for engaging with and being open to the past. Archival research, archaeology, re-construction, oral history and so forth, all have their own possibilities. The 'authenticity movement' in music, which aims to reconstruct instruments that were contemporary to the period in which a piece was composed and to play them in the manner in which they would then have been played, is one possible way of repeating that musical tradition.

Yet this kind of concern does not in and of itself make repetition 'authentic' in Heidegger's sense. For him 'authentic' repetition involves explicitly handing the past down to ourselves and enacting our world of significance for ourselves, rather than simply being influenced by the past. Historiologically accurate reproduction might be done so as to re-enact a world, or it might be done simply because that is assumed to be the best way to see what actually happened. So a reproduction or re-enactment that understands itself as 'historically accurate' can only be 'authentic' in Heidegger's sense if it does not take the results of historiological research as already established and its reproduction as a curiosity based upon those results, now available to all without the need for re-enactment on the part of those who take them up. It can be authentic if it understands itself as retrieving the past through a re-enactment of what is 'accurate' in historiological research. Historiology is now *our* tradition, it is a set of possibilities that we have given ourselves for engaging with and repeating the past. Not every retrieval of the past will be 'inauthentic' in Heidegger's sense simply because it does not engage in historical science, but any retrieval that does engage with these sciences can only be authentic if it is an attempt to re-enact and retrieve the very sense of being historically scientific for itself, rather than just receiving the results of its research and gathering it into an interesting collage.

Because Dasein is there with others, its tradition is something shared. Even if we can all create personal variations on traditions and have personal ways of repeating our own past as well as that of others, personal traditions are built from shared tradition and can in principle be shared by others. It follows from Dasein's existential structure of being-with that all 'historizing is co-historizing'.[18]

The difference between making a tradition authentically *our own* and inauthentically existing within the tradition is not a difference between what we do personally and what we do together. Rather it is the difference between simply inheriting what is passed down to us and positively handing down a tradition to ourselves and taking it over so as to make it our own.[19] Disturbingly, Heidegger's description of how this takes place contains a number of formulations that have since taken on highly charged significance, given the way that the historical situation was about to unfold in Germany after 1927 and the way that Heidegger himself became involved in National Socialism. He writes of becoming a people (*Volk*) free for its destiny (*Geschick*) in community and struggle (*Kampf*), and of such freedom allowing us to choose our heroes.[20] It is almost impossible to read these formulations without hearing in them echoes of the murderous inheritance that was to come. In the view of many, Heidegger became partly, if not wholly, complicit in the annexation of a significant heritage of thought, especially when he used some of these same formulations in his inaugural address upon being appointed rector of Freiburg University in 1933, 'The Self-Assertion of the German University'.[21]

What are we to do then when coming towards such a past? Unless we want to simply abandon it to that devastating inheritance, which Heidegger has been accused of doing, and thus re-enact such an abandonment, we need to retrieve it and to decide for ourselves if, when and how this thought became complicit. In this thinking complicity was perhaps made possible. For Heidegger there was no question of isolating life and thought, but only a question of how thought springs from life and then returns to it. When we retrieve the meaning of these words, at least as they were enacted in the writing of *Being and Time*, they do not seem to entirely abandon themselves in advance to that particular inheritance. The people are constituted not by determinate biological or cultural inheritance, but the sharing of a tradition that they actively take up. We are not simply born into a tradition, since a tradition is what we take up as our heritage from the inheritance we are thrown into. Struggle need not be a struggle against others, but a struggle with our own tendency to abandon ourselves to what 'everyone' understands, believes and does. Destiny cannot be the willed assumption of complete mastery and power over oneself and others, but is what is delivered to us by our tradition and thus indicates a necessary powerlessness at the heart of every ability and power that we take over from that tradition.[22] To choose a hero is to be enabled to choose those to whom we look for guidance and from whom we think we can learn, not to have somebody impose themselves upon us whose word is never to be questioned. That is not to say that Heidegger was in no way complicit in what was to come – he certainly was in various and sometimes horrendous ways, yet neither does it seem likely that he entirely and completely abandoned our whole philosophical inheritance to that particular heritage.

### iii. BEGINNING AGAIN WITH THE FIRST BEGINNING

This then is the being of history as Heidegger understood it in *Being and Time*: inheritance that we either uncritically allow to infuse and determine our thought and actions or which we take up explicitly and critically in a rejoinder with the past. Of course, it would be impossible to be completely and explicitly engaging with the full depth and dimensions of the inheritance that our thoughts and actions bear within them. Authentic historicality is a possibility of explicit engagement with our own openness to what has been, but it does not prevent us from being simply and constantly 'influenced'. We can become open to our own having been influenced, but that cannot mean that we become conscious of every influence and deliberately accept it or reject it. Rather, we can become open to the possibility of taking up or rejecting influences. Authentic historicality is a possibility that we give ourselves when we differentiate between our having been thrown into a situation and the task that we face in taking up the possibilities it affords us.

What is inherited and can be authentically repeated is not just what actually happened, but the horizon of possible significance within which it happened. That horizon of possible significance is the world of that Dasein, existing always together with others, for whom certain possibilities made sense, others did not, and yet others did not even arise. Implicit within an investigation into the sense of Dasein's historical existence, or the 'being of history', is therefore another kind of inquiry. In our historical existence and repetition of the meaningful worlds that have been, we may find that not only have there been changes in what is intelligible, but that the very way in which Dasein discloses an intelligible world has itself undergone transformation. That is precisely what Heidegger did come to think has been happening and in doing so he opens up an investigation into 'the history of being'. Coming to this investigation through his inquiry into the being of history, it was only in the 1930s that Heidegger began to explicitly formulate and reformulate a history of being. Nevertheless, the two inquiries would seem to mutually imply one another. An inquiry into the history of being must rely on an understanding, whether explicitly laid out or not, of the being of history, i.e., how it is that Dasein manages to open up and gain access to what has been. An inquiry into the being of history must rely on an understanding, whether explicitly laid out or not, of the history of being, i.e., how its own way of disclosing a meaningful world, including its own way of being open to the past, stands with regard to the disclosures that have already been.

The transformations that have taken place in the disclosure of the world, transformations traced in a history of being, are not understood by Heidegger as simple changes in the way that we view the world, changes in our 'world picture' or 'worldview'. That might imply that the world remains fundamentally the same and we simply develop different ways of looking at it. On the other hand, it might also imply that there is nothing to the world but the different subjective perspectives that people have on it. In an essay from 1938, 'The Age of the World Picture', Heidegger identifies this dilemma between objectivity and subjectivity in worldview as the result of the distinctive disclosure of the world that belongs to modernity. In modernity we understand ourselves as subjects who represent the world to themselves.[23] If we did not understand ourselves as subjects and the world as the representations of those subjects, then no such question of the subjectivity or objectivity of our representations arises. The difference between the modern world and the world of the Middle Ages is not between differing worldviews, but rather between fundamentally different ways in which the world is intelligible. In the Middle Ages the world was intelligible not as what was represented, whether subjective or objective, but as the creation of a Creator.[24] The transformation in the history of being could then be said to reflect back on our understanding of the being of history. In the Middle Ages historical change could not possibly have been understood as change in worldview, but only in terms of the revelatory history of God's creation. For us, including those of us who have faith in a creator

God, it is all but impossible not to understand this change in terms of a change in worldview.

Heidegger's inquiry into the history of being faces two potential objections even before one engages with its details. In the first place, it may be objected that the idea that there have been fundamental changes in the way that being is understood and the world is disclosed to us means that we are completely cut off from other ages or epochs in the history of being and can never understand them. This is clearly not what Heidegger concludes, since it would make the whole inquiry impossible. Rather, while he is at pains to point out that we constantly underestimate the differences between our world-disclosure and that of other epochs, Heidegger also frequently points out the ways in which the seeds of later world-disclosures are sown in those that precede them. So while the ancient Greeks in no way understood the world as composed of the representations of subjects, that world-disclosure was prepared by Plato's understanding of being as *eidos* (appearance/view).[25] Furthermore, we cannot understand the world of the ancient Greeks or the Middle Ages precisely as they understood it themselves, since that would require nothing less that becoming entirely ancient or medieval. But we can understand those worlds, even if sometimes with great difficulty, because they have not been utterly annihilated and replaced by our world, but have been transformed into our world. The modern world is not a simple variation on the ancient or medieval world, but there is a great deal of the ancient and medieval worlds that is received in it and open to repetition and re-enactment. The contrary objection might then be made that this thought of a history of being is reductive and simplistic, that it hinges on the idea of a single tradition running through 'Western civilization and metaphysics' that is untenably monolithic. It only gestures at difference and radical breaks, while trying to reduce history to a single uniform trajectory. Despite the precise attention to detail to be found in Heidegger's historical lecture courses, there are also very broad historical claims that pervade his work. These two lines of criticism do not in fact present Heidegger with an impossible dilemma for his 'history of being', but together they articulate precisely the dilemma that faces historical investigation as such. Any history must try to articulate what is essential to that tradition, period or occurrence that it is investigating, what makes it hang together as something to be inquired into. At the same time it must try to be as precise as possible about how that tradition, period or occurrence differentiates itself, how it gathers into itself a vast multiplicity of influences and trajectories and then disperses them again to be gathered up by others. Fundamental to any historical disclosure is this dilemma of gathering and dispersal of its own tradition.

Heidegger opens up extremely bold projections of the history of being. He does not shy away from trying to characterize guiding tendencies that have been taken up again and again throughout the tradition as we have inherited it. We have already come across his characterization of that whole history as onto-theology, an inquiry into the ground of being and the being of the ground. In *Contributions to Philosophy (from Enowning)* and other texts from the late 1930s, he begins to refer to this history as the 'first beginning'. The first beginning has unfolded into the whole of Western metaphysics and civilization, including the most 'anti-metaphysical' positivism and the globalized technological society that no longer belongs simply to 'the West'. The first beginning repeatedly begins by asking itself a 'guiding-question': 'what is a being? the question of beingness, being.'[26] It tries to move from its own understanding of beings to a thinking of what it is for anything to be at all. This first beginning may well end up, as has indeed been the case, becoming 'anti-metaphysical' and denying that there is a proper question here to be answered.[27] Heidegger, by contrast, suggests that when this guiding question properly understands itself it finds its ground in another question, the 'grounding-question': 'What is the truth of being?'[28] The guiding-question has, so to speak, narrowed the field from the start by taking as its guide beings as they are understood and thus that particular understanding or constellation of understanding of being that is already in place. The grounding-question asks about how that understanding of being or any other understanding of being takes place or comes about. It thus opens the field again for other understandings to take place. It is important that Heidegger does not call the return from the guiding-question to the grounding-question a 'second beginning', but rather 'another beginning'. Another beginning is not a new start from scratch, it is the attempt to think within the purview not of this understanding or that, but of that which brings about all understanding. We will not wake up one morning and find that another beginning has been instituted and the first beginning has been left behind. Another beginning is a return to the open field in which our understanding of being takes place and in which another, any other, understanding will also take place. It is a return to what Heidegger calls *Ereignis*, the 'event of appropriation' or 'enowning' in and through which understanding of being and the appearance of beings occurs.

At the beginning of the first beginning we usually place the Presocratic philosophers. Heidegger finds in their thinking the possibilities of an open field that has not yet been narrowed into a fixed understanding of what it is and must be for any being to be. At the same time he also finds there the possibility of posing the guiding-question, i.e., the thought that we can determine what it is for anything to be by taking beings as they are manifest to us as our guide. A return to the origin of philosophical thought does not necessarily involve turning to early Greek thinkers at all, but the retrieval of their thought can be and has been a significant way of reactivating our own thought. Such a repetition certainly does not involve claiming that everything we have learnt in the history of metaphysics has been an error and that the ancients had it right all along: 'Setting apart the other beginning from the first beginning can never have the sense of proving that the history of the guiding-question and thus "metaphysics" heretofore are an "error".'[29] Rather, we set apart another beginning by repeating the first beginning with renewed openness to what has been said there.

The return to origins, or the initiation of another beginning, is not something that can be achieved once and for all. It is not the return of ourselves and our thinking to a moment of pure potential that does not unfold in one way or another. Rather it is a return to what has been in a way that shows that it still harbors within it an origin that can unfold again and perhaps in other ways. As Heidegger puts it in a lecture course from 1937–1938, the same period that his was composing *Contributions to Philosophy*:

> In this way, the beginning contains in itself the unavoidable necessity that, in unfolding, it must surrender its originality. This does not speak against the greatness of the beginning but in favor of it. For, would what is great ever be great if it did not have to face up to the danger of collapse and did not have to succumb in its historical consequences to this danger, only to remain all the more illuminating in its initial singularity?[30]

This is philosophical thought's proper relation to its own origin. Not some hankering after a permanent state of innocence and pure undetermined possibility of thought that never actually thinks anything, but an understanding that as origins are unfolded they lose their singular openness. If we are able to find a way forward to that singularity again, then we may well develop other ways of thinking and disclosing the world that were never before thought possible.

## CHAPTER 10

# ART AND SCIENCE: POETRY AND THOUGHT

The poem of the understanding is philosophy. . . . Without philosophy a person remains divided in his most essential powers. He is two people – one who has understanding – and one who is a poet.

*Logological Fragments I*, 24

The idea that there are two cultures, two modes of intellectual inquiry, or more fundamentally two modes of thought and practice that belong to human existence, did not originate in 1959, when C. P. Snow delivered a public lecture at Cambridge University, *The Two Cultures and the Scientific Revolution*.[1] Snow's simplistic view of the failure of 'literary intellectuals' to appreciate natural science does nevertheless begin to point towards divisions that permeate our understanding of culture and thought. The roots of such divisions go very deep into our heritage, receiving many different formulations and precipitating many attempts at reconciliation. These divides and reconciliations permeate our view not only of academic and intellectual inquiry, but also our very conception of what it means to be a thinking being.

In 1959, the year of Snow's address, Heidegger published a collection of lectures and essays that would seem to place him firmly and irretrievably on the 'literary' and artistic side of any division in the range of thought and experience. *On the Way to Language* includes numerous reflections on the poetry of such figures as Stefan George, Georg Trakl and Friedrich Hölderlin. These poems elucidate the poetic experience of language that Heidegger had come to think underlies all of our linguistic and reflective abilities, but which we constantly ignore or cover over. Such experiences point us among other things towards our non-mastery of language, the point at which words fail us, the depth of meaning that our words are invested with that is beyond our complete control. Thus Heidegger claims that for all we think that it is we who put language to use as an instrument for our purposes, the poetic experience of language requires a listening to language, as 'language speaks', and we speak by listening to and responding to what has been spoken.[2]

Does this reflection on poetic experience with language mean that Heidegger had abandoned thought? Such a conclusion might stem from the idea that real thought occurs in science. Heidegger, however, claims that poetry and art must not be relegated to decorative and whimsical pastimes, if we are to think through the way that science and technology have come about and what their true significance is. He had come to this thought over a long period of reflection on the relations between philosophy, art and science.

## i. UNDERMINING THE ACADEMIC DIVIDE

When Heidegger was a student and young academic philosopher in early twentieth-century Germany, there was a deep-seated sense that there were two cultures of thought, or two kinds of 'science'. On the one hand, there are the natural sciences (*Naturwissenschaften*) that try to find universal laws of nature and generally applicable explanations for natural phenomena. On the other hand, there are the 'spiritual sciences' (*Geisteswissenschaften*), which in English are usually called humanities, that seem to be concerned with phenomena that cannot be easily brought under such laws and general explanations, but rather are concerned with the particularities of texts, actions, works and so forth. How was philosophy to situate itself with regard to these two cultures? Does philosophy belong to one or the other? Are they really irreconcilable, or is there actually a way of finding what is common between them?

These were the kind of questions that were felt to be philosophically pressing. There were two schools of thought that tried to engage with them. On the whole, the neo-Kantians saw philosophy as principally engaged in giving a conceptual grounding to the natural sciences. The historical and hermeneutic school, on the other hand, thought that we must ultimately grasp the significance of natural science within an understanding of the history and development of human knowledge and life as such. These two philosophical schools did not always simply concentrate all their efforts on the one side of this distinction between sciences with which they had greatest affinity. Rather, each tried to encompass the other by devising a philosophical method that could recognize and do justice to differences within the whole of human knowledge, while at the same time maintaining that knowledge as a unified whole. In particular the Baden school of neo-Kantianism, which included Heinrich Rickert (1863–1936), who supervised Heidegger's doctoral dissertation, and Wilhelm Windelband (1848–1915), tried to devise a transcendental approach to historical and human sciences, claiming that while such knowledge is not a search for general laws like the natural sciences, it could work out a theory of human values and 'types' that does justice to the particularity that these sciences are interested in, yet still allow them to become universally grounded sciences.[3] These ideas had an enormous influence on the early development of social sciences, including Max Weber (1864–1920), who employed a similar concept of 'ideal type' in his sociological and historical studies.[4] Wilhelm Dilthey (1833–1911), on the other hand, had developed a set of concepts that was to have an enormous influence on the development of historical and social science as well as Heidegger's philosophical thought. He hoped to understand the distinction between the natural sciences and the 'spiritual sciences', in terms of what they are trying to achieve. While the natural sciences aim at the *explanation* of natural events in terms of universal laws, the spiritual sciences aim at the *understanding* of human action in history. Understanding cannot ultimately be reached through a theory of intellectual cognition alone, but must involve us in the whole historical world of experience and understanding within which that human action that we want to understand takes place.[5]

The young Heidegger was at the heart of these concerns and debates as he developed his own style of thinking and attempted to unify our thought and experience of nature and history. He had taken courses in both the natural and the spiritual sciences as a student and like his philosophical mentors he was keen to try to understand both the differences and the possible unity of these modes of thought and experience. In an important early essay from 1915, 'The Concept of Time in the Science of History', he had already focused on *time* as the key to this enterprise. There he sharply distinguishes the concept of time employed in physics and that employed in history and concludes that the recognition of this 'complete otherness vis-à-vis the concept of time' is crucial for gaining a better understanding of historical science.[6] A decade later in an essay on 'Wilhelm Dilthey's Research and the Struggle for a Historical Worldview', Heidegger was developing his ontology of Dasein, including the idea that temporalization is the fundamental way in which we inhabit our world, and he offers criticisms of the neo-Kantian development of Dilthey's project. If we are able to get past the idea that theoretical cognitive knowledge grounds all of our understanding rather than being a part the way we understand and are in the world, then we will find our own existence to be a temporality that essentially involves historicality. Heidegger radicalized Dilthey's conception of understanding, so that our temporalizing understanding is what allows us to be in the world in any way at all. Theoretical inquiry whether in 'natural' or 'spiritual' science, is derived from that. This understanding is, however, necessarily caught up in certain limits: 'This possibility is determined by how we ourselves understand and define our own Dasein.'[7] Without underestimating or ignoring the radical distinctions between the natural and historical sciences that he had previously identified, without wishing to reconcile them by reducing one to the other, Heidegger hoped that an ontology of Dasein would undermine these differences in the sense of uncovering the temporalizing understanding that makes both of these modes of thought and experience possible. Significantly, at the end of this 1925 essay, Heidegger hints at research that he has been conducting into the ancients, suggesting that at the root of these controversies concerning the distinction between two modes of inquiry is a repetition of what had already been articulated in antiquity.[8]

## ii. RETURNING THE ARTS AND SCIENCES TO THEMSELVES

In the winter semester of 1924–1925, Heidegger had delivered a lecture course on Plato's dialogue *The Sophist*. In the event he actually spent a very substantial preliminary part of the course discussing Aristotle, especially parts of the *Nichomachean Ethics* and *Metaphysics*. He argues that it is in Aristotle that we find a clarification and articulation of the original unified field of *logos* and *alētheuein*, discursive showing and disclosive truth, that Plato had opened up as a field of research. Heidegger wants to return us to that field, in the question of 'being', that is developed in *Being and Time*. However, the articulation of discourse and truth that Aristotle provides us with becomes the root of the divisions of thought and experience that pervade our tradition, right down to the various positing of two cultures of science and art, natural science and human science, and so forth. Heidegger's reconstruction of Aristotle's articulation, beginning with book 6 of the *Nichomachean Ethics*, turns upon a distinction between two basic modes of disclosing the truth, those that are *epistēmonikon* and those that are *logistikon*. The first is that mode which can contribute to and develop into knowledge. The second is that which considers and contributes to deliberation.[9] Here we see the germ of the distinction that will harden into the difference between theory and practice that still pervades our self-understanding.

There is, however, a further distinction to be taken into account in Heidegger's reconstruction of Aristotle's articulation of the field. For the disclosive mode of *epistēmonikon* is further divided into *epistēmē* and *sophia*, while the mode of *logistikon* is divided into *technē* and *phronēsis*. Heidegger's translations of these terms depart from those in normal usage and shed some light on how he understands their relation to more contemporary divisions of our modes of disclosive existence. *Epistēmē*, frequently translated simply as 'knowledge', is here translated as 'science' (*Wissenschaft*). *Sophia*, frequently translated as 'wisdom', Heidegger translates as 'understanding' (*Verstehen*). *Sophia* for him is thus related to the mode of being that Dilthey thought of as underpinning the 'spiritual sciences' and which Heidegger himself radicalizes into the understanding of being that makes possible every ability that we have to be in the world. *Technē*, usually translated as 'art', 'skill' or 'craft', here becomes 'know-how (in taking care, manipulating, producing)' and *phronēsis*, traditionally translated as 'practical wisdom' is retrieved as 'circumspection (insight) (*Umsicht, Einsicht*)'.[10] Clearly these articulations also find their way into Heidegger's analysis of Dasein's way of being-in-the-world, which for the most part is simply tackling its environment, but which can also achieve insight into the temporalization that makes this possible.

The original disclosive truth of Dasein's existence, its *alētheuein*, is thus unfolded by Aristotle into a twofold and then a fourfold distinction between modes of disclosure. Heidegger thought we can return to the unity of these modes in the unconcealing disclosure of truth and show that our understanding of disclosure has been distorted by picking up particular aspects of this clarifying unfolding and identifying them with disclosure itself. In our subsequent history there has been a tendency to take one mode as being the primary and sometimes even the only proper mode of disclosure, grounding all the others. *Epistēmē*, for example, which Heidegger has translated as 'science', was concerned with beings 'that always are' linking it to a conception of time as 'constant presence' or 'eternity' (*aei*).[11] This is a derivative concept of time that represents everything as present and theoretically open to view, a conception that derives from the original temporalization by which Dasein discloses its world. Science looks for what is constantly and universally applicable. To the extent that this mode of disclosure is given priority over every other kind and even represented as the only mode that properly discloses, we are in the grip of an epistemic distortion of truth.

Even before any attempt to return to the original breadth and unity of disclosure, Aristotle's clarificatory distinctions afford us the opportunity to return distinct modes of disclosure to a better understanding of themselves than any straightforward distinction between science and art, or theory and practice, allows for. For according to Heidegger's interpretation, the distinction of the mode of *epistēmonikon* into *epistēmē* and *sophia* and of *logistikon* into *technē* and *phronēsis*, allows us to see a crucial difference within these modes of disclosure not as to *what* they disclose but as to *how* they disclose. Understanding (*sophia*) is not some capacity separate from science (*epistēmē*), but an epistemic disclosure that relates itself to what science must always presuppose, its origins (*archai* – usually translated in this context as 'principles'), in the sense of what allows it to disclose in this way. Understanding is thus genuine, proper or authentic 'science' because it relates itself to its own disclosive origin. Similarly, within the realm of the *logistikon*, circumspective insight (*phronēsis*) is not some distinct capacity to know-how (*technē*), but genuine, proper or authentic know-how because it relates itself to the origins that know-how must presuppose but does not relate itself to.[12] Circumspective insight is thus genuine, proper or authentic 'art' or 'skill'.

Aristotle thus pursues two directions of questioning with regard to the whole range of Dasein's thought and experience: '[A]t first he asks about the beings which are to be disclosed; then he raises the question of whether the respective *alētheuein* [disclosure] also discloses the *archē* [origin] of those beings. The second question is always the criterion for determining whether the *alētheuein* is a genuine one or not.'[13] It is the second line of questioning, usually fully eclipsed by the first, that Heidegger thinks of as a phenomenological inquiry into *how* beings are disclosed in their being. The ability to distinguish a genuine or authentic mode of disclosure, that reflects upon its own origins in disclosure itself, from an ungenuine or inauthentic mode that does not, is ultimately of far more importance than the ability to separate modes of disclosure on the basis of what they are trying to disclose. We should be more concerned about whether our practice of arts and sciences is genuinely reflective in this way than with the characterization, evaluation and quantification of the artefacts and results that they produce. It is only with that genuine reflection on the origins of our practice that those artefacts brought about by skill or art and those results produced by science are not simply objects for producing momentary pleasure or means to overcome immediate challenges and problems, but contribute towards building and cultivating a world of disclosure through a full range of reflective arts and sciences.

### iii. THE CULT(URE) OF TECHNOLOGY

Over the course of his philosophical career Heidegger became more and more convinced that our inherited mode of disclosure is predominantly technical and that even *epistēmē* has been subordinated to the technical, to 'know-how', that takes care of itself in manipulation and production.

In *The Basic Problems of Phenomenology* he begins to argue that metaphysics itself is a feature of the technical and productive understanding of disclosure. It is a 'productivist metaphysics'. Production involves having a set idea in advance of the product that is to be produced. This is something that the Greeks first understood about production. We have inherited a productivist mode of disclosure from a broader range of unveiling and disclosive existence which had already begun to focus on *technē* and the productive comportment of Dasein as *the* way to understand all the modes of disclosure and the being of beings itself. The basic concepts of Greek ontology are inflected by a predominantly productive comportment that comes to include nature itself, *phusis*, stemming from the verb *phuein*: 'Phuein means to let grow, procreate, engender, produce, primarily to produce itself.'[14] Even that kind of being which is supposed to be supremely independent, *ousia*, usually translated as 'substance', is understood in terms of a predominantly technical and productive comportment, because it is a product of itself that stands by itself and lies before us at our disposal.[15] It is easy to see how this idea that the being of things is primarily production was joined on to the Christian idea that everything is created by God. More difficult is Heidegger's claim that in modernity, even where we have abandoned the idea that all things have been created or produced by God, our idea of being still derives from a predominantly productive stance, precisely because what is produced becomes independent of the producer. A product is complete in itself and no longer attached to its producer. Thus, one of the surprising results of a productivist metaphysics is that it leads us to think of things not as always related to us, but as fundamentally independent: 'The being that is *understood in productive comportment* is exactly *the being-in-itself of the product.*'[16] Furthermore, production discovers what is independent from the producer as what is 'already-there' and which lends itself to the production or resists it. It is in that way that productive comportment encounters 'independent' nature.[17]

Our very understanding of being is one dominated by the technical and productive mode of disclosure. In *Contributions to Philosophy* Heidegger develops this thought, claiming that we are in the grip of a predominately technical understanding of being as 'machination': 'Machination is the domination of making and what is made.'[18] This does not entail the belief that everything is a product or construct of human making, but is rather a general understanding of the being of all beings in terms of making and self-making. This understanding has resulted in the extraordinary expansion of human productivity that is one of the central features of the age of technology. This is also a matter of how we view our own being. The being of all beings is predominantly understood in terms of making and production, and we come to understand ourselves in that way too. We can think of the way Marx understood the 'species-being' of human beings as socially productive activity, an idea that led to the devastating misapprehension that human communal life could simply be manipulated at will. The capitalist understanding of human beings that now dominates almost everywhere is of producer-consumers, producing to consume and producing consumption.

That Dasein's understanding of being and the disclosure of being becomes 'machination' is of far more significance than distinctions between different sciences. Within university research, institutional operation and production means that the 'now current differentiation into historical and experimental-exact sciences' and the distinction between the natural and the human or 'spiritual' sciences, although helpful in guiding thinking about how science itself should be characterized, is now understood by Heidegger to be 'only superficial and actually only imperfectly covers the uniform essence of the seemingly very different sciences.'[19] A further distinctive feature of the dominance of the technical productive understanding of being is that we understand our cultural lives in general in terms of 'lived experience'. This term no longer designates that textured engagement with the world that the young Heidegger had hoped phenomenology would allow us to bring to the fore. That very experience has become something that is produced by and for us and that we expect to produce particular psychological results in us.[20] There is huge diversity of experience, but what really counts is a great monoculture of productivity. Our understanding of culture itself is drawn into machination, becoming the production and consumption of lived experiences that was dubbed a little later by Theodor Adorno and Max Horkheimer the 'culture industry'.[21] Scientific and scholarly research of all kinds are plugged into this productivity and are allowed to 'retain the last remnant of a *cultural decoration* only as long as for the time being they must continue to be the instrument of "culture-oriented political" propaganda'.[22]

Later still, in the 1953 essay 'The Question Concerning Technology', Heidegger tries to indicate the breadth and scale of the dominance of technical disclosure. It is not just a question of making or producing things in the usual sense, but also of how we perceive and think about everything in the world. He uses the term *Ge-stell* to try to gather together all of these different features and show their inner unity.[23] At the heart of modern technology lies a variety of different kinds of 'positing' (*stellen*), including representative thinking (*vorstellen*), producing (*herstellen*) and ordering (*bestellen*). These different kinds of positing are gathered together (the prefix 'Ge' frequently designates the gathering together of a diverse range of phenomena as Heidegger points out) and unfolded within a dominant attitude towards the world that is set up before us and ordered in such a way that everything is 'challenged' to reveal itself and made into a stock or standing-reserve of potential that is set out in advance.[24]

Heidegger's thinking of the dominance of technical disclosure can and has led many to the conclusion that he was one of the literary 'natural luddites' that Snow so despised. It is telling that the term 'luddite' has come to refer to someone who has a blanket and nonsensical hatred of any kind of technical innovation. The luddites were not simply haters of technology, but a social movement that responded to a particular manifestation of technological disclosure that they saw as inappropriate and oppressive. However, what is essential to technological disclosure as Heidegger understands it is not the use of machines, products or innovations of any distinctive kind. As a way of disclosing the world which involves *setting up* the world of all possibilities for representation, production and consumption, technology in Heidegger's sense is what brings about the use of machines and technological systems. Heidegger did not think that we could or should simply do away with machines and technological innovations. He did think that it is imperative that we learn to *freely* respond to technological disclosure, that is, the way that the world reveals itself to us as something that is set up in various ways.

Heidegger's first intention was to show us that we are far more deeply rooted in technological disclosure than we usually realize. It does not just form one aspect of our lives and understanding of the world around us, but *forms and posits* that whole world. It reveals a danger that has not been fully realized: 'The coming of the presence of technology threatens revealing, threatens it with the possibility that all revealing will be consumed in ordering and that everything will be present only in the standing-reserve. Human activity can never directly counter this danger.'[25] However, this does not mean that we can simply do nothing at all. If, for example, we can begin to open up technical disclosure onto its own broader heritage, then we may find possibilities for interactive disclosure of the world other than those prescribed and set up at present.

To describe what Heidegger saw as the danger and the potential 'saving power' in technology, we might say that it is in danger of becoming a cult, in the modern sense of an unreflective worship and devotion that absorbs us completely and prescribes to us our every possibility. The word 'cult', however, has the same roots as 'culture', in the Latin *cultus*, care, cultivation, worship, from *colere*, to tend, guard, cultivate or till. Heidegger hoped that the positing, challenging and ordering of technological disclosure could be turned into cultivation. What he called for and tried to help us prepare the way for might be called *appropriate* disclosure, a turning about of the technical disclosure that tries to set up and prescribe what is appropriate in every case. Appropriate disclosure can only come about through free response in each case. 'Appropriate technology' in that sense would not simply involve designating what kinds of devices, products, procedures and operations are appropriate and which are not in every case. One cannot technically order what is appropriate because it requires responsiveness to what is unique and never set up in advance. One cannot demand or require such responsiveness to what is appropriate, one can only demand or require a designated set of responses. If we find ourselves able to respond appropriately in and through our own technically dominated disclosure of the world, this response will not be something that can be demanded or prescribed in advance.

#### iv. TWO CULTURES IN ONE

To this way of thinking we are never completely in control of the way that the world is disclosed to us, but neither are we ever completely subjected to it as it happens to be. We are intimately and inextricably involved in the disclosure that takes place through the whole range of ways in which we are in the world, ways that we never have completely at our disposal. That being the case, if there is to be appropriate disclosure then it will certainly require certain ways of conducting ourselves.

Two kinds of conduct that Heidegger thought of as possible ways of preparing for appropriate disclosure are reflective thought and poetry. Technological disclosure recognizes only thought that can establish, calculate and predict in advance. It recognizes poetry and all art forms as the occasion for interesting aesthetic distraction, as a sector of cultural enterprise.[26] The thought and poetry that

Heidegger thinks might turn around technological disclosure are quite different. To understand the difference we can turn to what is involved in culture and cultivation. One understanding of cultivating the intellect, in fact of education in general, is: 'to set up a preformed model (*Vor-bild*) and to set forth a preestablished rule (*Vor-schrift*)'.[27] This is a technical and productive conception of education, a key feature of production being that it sets up in advance an image, form or plan of what it is that it wants to produce: 'Cultivating the intellect requires a guiding image rendered secure in advance, as well as a standing-ground fortified on all sides.'[28] However, what cannot be set up in advance is how this particular 'image' of what is to be produced in culture and education comes about, such that it can be set up as a guide. Reflective thought is a kind of cultivation that differs from setting up a model and allows these models and prescriptions to come about in the first place. Reflective thought does not require that we cease production, and that we stop planning or calculating what is to come in advance. It requires that in the midst of production we are careful in our preparation of what we have been given to make that production possible and that in challenging it to produce what is set up in advance we do not exhaust it completely.

What about poetry? The Greek word *poēsis* was not confined to the composition of verse, but signified any kind of production, creation or bringing about of an artefact or event. Aristotle distinguishes between making (*poēsis*) and acting (*praxis*),[29] arguing that the former is directed towards a production beyond itself while the latter is not. *Technē*, art, skill or what Heidegger called 'know-how', is thus a kind of making, but making is here thought of in terms of production that has the form of what it wants to produce set up in advance. Heidegger, however, understands poetry in a sense still broader than this. It is not confined to the composition of verse, nor even to productive making, nor finally even to an active 'praxis'. Already in his 1935 lecture, 'The Origin of the Work of Art' Heidegger understood poetry not as a special kind of art, but as the truth of all art: 'Poetry is the saying of the unconcealment of beings.'[30]

Heidegger actually reserves the German word derived from the Greek *Poesie*, poesy, for the composition of verse, while the word *Dichtung*, deriving from the Latin 'dictare', to say repeatedly, dictate, compose, comes to mean for him the whole range of disclosure that can take place in any art that opens the world. It is this very unconcealing of a world that has become dominated by productive activity. What is distinctive about technical disclosure is that it recognizes no limit to what can be represented, produced and challenged to make its appearance in some way and thus does not recognize itself as limiting the range of ways in which a world can be disclosed.

So the cultivation of reflective thought does not require that we cease to produce models of thought, but reflects upon that which cannot be fully grasped by any model, our very potential for disclosing the world. Reflective thought enables us to respond freely to what our models of thought cannot represent. Poetic experience requires us to respond to what is not fully at our disposal in production. If we are not completely set on producing to a scheme that is set up in advance, then in the midst of producing we can uncover what was totally unexpected. We can allow ourselves to respond to the unexpected, instead of automatically seeing it as hindrance to the production of what we set out to bring about. Reflective thought and poetry are far from identical, but they are united in this, that they both respond to what cannot be set out in advance or fully grasped in its own thought and work.

What is it that cannot be set out from the start or fully grasped? In one of the essays in his 1959 collection *On the Way to Language* Heidegger says that thinking and poetry belong together as different ways of responding to the Saying that neither can fully comprehend: 'From Saying it comes to pass that World is made to appear.'[31] The world comes to pass through thought and poetry as it responds to what has been said and draws out what that saying itself did not expect. Technical and calculative thinking not only cannot get a grip on this opening-saying that allows all phenomena to appear; it does not even recognize itself as a response to it. Reflective thinking and poetry are ways of responding that cannot be produced, manipulated or set up in advance. Nevertheless, there is potentially a reflective and poetic moment in every productive activity and calculation. In the midst of every productive activity that knows roughly where it is going in advance there is the possibility of encountering what was not expected. The two cultures of art and science start out in and return to the cultivation of poetry and reflective thought. These two ways of responding, however different, are united in their responsiveness to what is unexpected and startling. Heidegger himself was startled by the possibility of responsiveness that finds the unexpected even in what is established and received. He sought to startle us too into a response.

# NOTES

## INTRODUCTION

1. Friedrich Nietzsche, 'The Wanderer and His Shadow', in *On the Genealogy of Morals* and *Ecce Homo*, trans. Walter Kaufmann (New York: Vintage, 1969), 180.
2. EGT 60–64.
3. BT 220/262.
4. Maurice Merleau-Ponty, *Nature: Course Notes from the Collège de France*, trans. Robert Vallier (Evanston: Northwestern University Press, 2003), 87.

## CHAPTER 1: PHENOMENOLOGY: THE LOGIC OF APPEARING

1. IPR 34–35/44–47.
2. Edmund Husserl, 'Philosophy as a Rigorous Science' in Peter McCormick and Frederick A. Elliston (eds), *Husserl: Shorter Works*, (Notre Dame, Indiana: University of Notre Dame Press, 1981), 196.
3. Heidegger's first doctoral thesis, submitted in 1913 was entitled 'Theory and Judgement in Psychologism: Critical and Positive Contributions to Logic'. His post-doctoral degree 'The Theory of Categories and Meaning in Duns Scotus', obtained in 1915, dealt with two scholastic sources (one of which was later discovered to have been authored by Thomas of Erfurt) in the light of contemporary problems in philosophy of logic.
4. Edmund Husserl, *Ideas Pertaining to a Pure Phenomenology and to Phenomenological Philosophy, First Book*, trans. Fred Kersten (Dordrecht: Kluwer, 1998), 56–57.
5. Husserl, *Ideas Pertaining to a Pure Phenomenology*, 57–58 and Part Two, Chapter 4 passim.
6. HCT 113/154.
7. HCT 107/147.

8. Heidegger explicitly argues for this 'one world' reading of Kant, which has more recently been championed by Henry Allison. KPM 22–3/31–34. cf. Henry E. Allison, *Kant's Transcendental Idealism: An Interpretation and Defence*, 2nd edn (New Haven: Yale University Press, 2004), 16.
9. CPR B 69.
10. Edmund Husserl, *Logical Investigations*, Vol II, trans. J. N. Findlay (London: Routledge, 2001), 280–24. See, HCT § 6.
11. KPM 25–26/37.
12. KPM 98/139–140.
13. KPM 95–96/136–137.
14. KPM 67/95.
15. KPM 112–120/160–172.
16. TDP 96/114.
17. PRL 41–42/60–61.
18. PRL 40–41/59.
19. KPM 67/95.
20. PIA 22/27–28.
21. PIA 27/33.
22. FCM 291–300/421–435.
23. BT 58/34.
24. IPR 27/36.

## CHAPTER 2: DASEIN: A LIVING QUESTION

1. BT 26–27/7.
2. BT 24/7.
3. BT 68/43.
4. OHF 29–30/36–37.
5. OHF 32–34/40–43.
6. OHF 11/15.
7. OHF 15/20.
8. BT 33/12.
9. PIA 66/87.
10. BT 28/8.
11. BT 34/13.
12. OHF 12/15.
13. BT 174/135.
14. MFL 136/172.
15. MFL 137/172.
16. MFL 137/172–3.
17. There is significant debate over the tenability of Heidegger's thought of the 'neutrality' of Dasein. One of the first to draw attention to this

problem was Jacques Derrida, who argued that 'neutrality' has the potential to call into question even such basic tenets of our understanding of sexual embodiment as the duality of the sexes. See Jacques Derrida, 'Geschlecht: sexual difference, ontological difference' in *Research in Phenomenology* (Vol. 13, No.1, 1983) 65–83.

18. BT 74–75/48–49.
19. BT 75/50.
20. BT 68/42.
21. Supplements 163.
22. BCAP 16/21.
23. FCM 184/272.
24. FCM 255/371–2.
25. FCM 259/377.

## CHAPTER 3: WORLD: THE EVENT OF MEANING

1. BT 249/205.
2. BT 64–65/93.
3. BT 79/54.
4. BT 97/68.
5. BT 98/69.
6. BT 69/98.
7. BT 97/68.
8. BT 98/69 Terms that Macquarrie and Robinson translate as 'totality', such as, 'equipmental totality', 'referential totality' and so forth, are usually better translated as 'whole', since a totality is made up of a complete collection of items, while the point here is that the whole is prior to any individual items.
9. BT 100/70.
10. BT 119/86. The Macquarrie and Robinson translation does not generally bring to the fore the important point that this whole must already be in place when we encounter things and that we thus encounter them 'on the basis' of the whole.
11. BT 120/87.
12. BT 99/70. See note 8 above.
13. BT 112/81.
14. BT 114/82.
15. BT 99/69.
16. BT 102–103/73.
17. BT 103/73.
18. BT 103/74.
19. BT 117/85.
20. BT 97/68.

21. BT 99/70.
22. BT 116–117/84.
23. Michel Haar, *The Song of the Earth: Heidegger and the Grounds of the History of Being*, trans. Reginald Lilly (Bloomington: Indiana University Press, 1993), 19.
24. TDP 38/46.
25. TDP 39/46.
26. TDP 61/73.
27. TDP 63–64/75.
28. See, OHF 78–80/101–104. BT §41 argues that care is the primordial being of Dasein and §65 argues that it must be ontologically understood as temporality.

## CHAPTER 4: ANYONE AND EVERYONE

1. BT 157–8/121–2. Macquarrie and Robinson translate '*Fürsorge*,' caring-for, as 'solicitude,' which tends to conceal the etymological link to care (*Sorge*).
2. This threefold distinction has particular prominence in the lecture course Heidegger held in the winter semester of 1919–1920. See, Theodore Kiesel, *The Genesis of Being and Time* (Berkeley: University of California Press, 1993), 117–123.
3. BPP 171/243.
4. BPP 172–173. As the translator Albert Hofstadter notes, the cited passage can be found in *The Notebooks of Malte Laurids Brigge*, trans. M. D. Herter Norton (New York: Norton, 1949) 46 ff.
5. BT 156–157/120.
6. BCAP 45/64.
7. The translation of 'das Man' as the 'They' used by Macquarrie and Robinson has the advantage of connecting the phenomenon in question to English idioms which exemplify it, such as 'They say X', 'So they say' etc. However, it is potentially misleading insofar as it suggests that I myself am not a part of this anonymous 'they'.
8. BT 165/127.
9. BT 163–164/126.
10. BT 164/126.
11. BT 164/126.
12. BT 167/129.
13. BT 164/126.
14. BT 165/128.
15. *Supplements* 164.
16. BT 166/128.
17. BT 167/129.

18. BPP 171/243. Cf, BT 130/168.
19. BCAP 45/64.
20. BT 275–276/232 (translation modified).

CHAPTER 5: FINDING ONESELF IN A MOOD

1. BT 175/136.
2. BT 178/138–139.
3. BT 172 ff /134 ff. Macquarrie and Robinson here translate 'Befind-lichkeit' as 'state-of-mind', but 'disposition' is now the usual translation. State-of-mind suggests a subjective feeling that might be unrelated to circumstance and a static attitude, which are quite contrary to the sense of disposition as Heidegger understands it.
4. BT 182/142–3.
5. Attunement is now frequently used to translate Heidegger's term.
6. BT § 30.
7. BT 179–82/140–2.
8. Ludwig Wittgenstein, *Tractatus Logico-Philosophicus*, trans. C. K. Ogden (London: Routledge, 1996) 6.43.
9. BT 230/185.
10. BT 230/186.
11. BT 233/188–189 Here Heidegger points out that he selects this term for no other reason than that the German term 'Unheimlich' means literally 'not-at-home'.
12. BT 231/187.
13. BT 232/188.
14. PM 88/112.
15. PM 110/87.
16. FCM § 21.
17. FCM § 24.
18. FCM 134/202.
19. FCM § 33.
20. FCM 151/227 An excellent study of the phenomenon of boredom that places Heidegger's analysis into a larger philosophical and cultural context and gives a sympathetic but critical reading of him on this point is Lars Svendsen's *The Philosophy of Boredom*, trans. John Irons (London: Reacktion Books, 2005).
21. WM 87/110.
22. WM 93/118.
23. FCM 77/115.
24. BT 235/190 note iv and FCM 150/225.
25. See Søren Kierkegaard, *The Concept of Anxiety*, trans. Reidar Thomte with Albert B. Anderson (Princeton: Princeton University Press, 1980)

and *Sickness unto Death*, trans. Howard V. Hong and Edna H. Hong (Princeton: Princeton University Press, 1980).
26. FCM 60/91.

## CHAPTER 6: MEANING AND TRUTH

1. BT 110/80.
2. BT 193/152.
3. BT 194/153.
4. BT 210/166.
5. BT 194/152.
6. BT 191/150.
7. BT189/149.
8. BT 189/149.
9. BT 188/148.
10. R. G. Collingwood, *An Autobiography* (Oxford: Oxford University Press, 1978), 132. I am grateful to Jonas Ahlskog for pointing me towards this passage.
11. BT esp. § 44.
12. BT 185/145.
13. MFL 208/269.
14. WM 136/179.
15. The German term 'Entsclossenheit', 'resolute disclosure' is translated by Macquarrie and Robinson as 'resoluteness' BT 343/ 297. Although they point out the connection between 'Entschlossenheit' and 'Erschlossenheit' in a footnote, the crucial significance of that connection tends to get lost. The phenomenon in question is a kind of disclosure that takes place through being resolved.
16. Friedrich Nietzsche, *The Gay Science*, trans. Walter Kaufmann (New York: Vintage, 1974) § 344.
17. FCM 204/300.
18. BT 263/221.
19. BT 265/222.
20. BT 263/220.
21. BT 262/219.
22. BPP 216/308.
23. CP 245/351.
24. BT 265/222.
25. WM 171/129.
26. WM 179/139–140.
27. OBT 25/36.
28. CP 273/391.

## CHAPTER 7: TIME AND SPACE

1. I use the term 'ruler-space' here as a counterpart to the 'clock-time' that Heidegger analyses in some detail. See, e.g., BT §81.
2. BT 138/105.
3. BT 139/105.
4. BT 143/108.
5. BT 145/111.
6. BT 146/111.
7. BT 146/111.
8. PLT 165.
9. BT 19/1.
10. CPR A30/B46-A 49/B66, The 'Transcendental Aesthetic', second section 'On Time'.
11. CPR B274- B279, The 'Refutation of Idealism'.
12. CPR A137/B176- A147/ B187, 'On the schematism of pure concepts of the understanding'.
13. Henri Bergson, *Creative Evolution*, trans. Arthur Mitchell (Mineola, New York: Dover, 1998) esp. 1–7 and 204–208.
14. Bergson is mentioned a number of times in *Being and Time*, usually to assert that despite appearances his concept of time is still wedded to the 'ordinary conception'. Somewhat more extended discussion can be found in MFL 206–2077/267–268.
15. Edmund Husserl, *The Phenomenology of Internal Time-Consciousness*, trans. James C. Churchill (Bloomington: Indiana University Press, 1964). In 1926 when Heidegger was finishing the manuscript of *Being and Time* Husserl entrusted him with the task of editing these lectures and bringing them to publication. A great deal of work had already been done on the manuscript by Husserl's former assistant Edith Stein.
16. BT 377/329.
17. BT 377/328.
18. BT 375/327.
19. BT 378/329.
20. BT 427/375.
21. BT 473/421, A more standard translation of the definition is 'number of motion with respect to "before" and "after."' Aristotle, *Physics* 219b1.
22. See, e.g., *Nichomachean Ethics* book VI. Heidegger comments that Aristotle fails to adequately connect his analysis of *kairos* with what he otherwise understands by time as 'now', BPP 288/409.
23. BT 388/338.
24. Heidegger mentions Kierkegaard's penetrating analysis of the 'moment of vision' in *Being and Time* (footnote iii, to BT 388/338), but criticizes him for sticking to the ordinary conception of time and describing

it in terms of 'now' and 'eternity.' He produces an important reading of the 'moment of vision' in Nietzsche's thinking of time much later in his lecture courses on Nietzsche. See, N1 'The Vision and the Riddle'.

25. BT 418/368 & 472/419.
26. BT 472/419.
27. BT 347/300.
28. BT §70.
29. CP 259/371 (translation modified).
30. CP 263/241.
31. CP 270/378.
32. PLT 221/VA 190.

## CHAPTER 8: WAYS OF LIFE AND DEATH

1. BT 320/258.
2. BT 275/232.
3. BT 276/233.
4. BT 291/247.
5. BT 290/246.
6. BT 289/245.
7. Samuel Beckett, *Three Occasional Pieces* (London: Faber and Faber, 1982) 11.
8. BT 303/259.
9. BT 280/236.
10. BT 282/238.
11. BT 287/243.
12. BT 288/244.
13. BT 289/244–245.
14. BT 284/240.
15. BT 309/264.
16. BT 302/258.
17. BT 299/255.
18. BT 302/258.
19. BT 292/248.
20. BT 311/268.
21. BT 320/275.
22. BT 318/273.
23. BT 320/275.
24. BT 334/288.
25. BT 329/283.
26. BT 330/284.
27. BT 331/285.

28. Supplements 169.
29. BT 332/286.
30. Friedrich Nietzsche, *On the Genealogy of Morals* and *Ecce Homo*, translated by Walter Kaufmann (New York: Vintage, 1969) Essay 2 § 21.
31. BT 340/294.
32. BT 355/307.
33. The phrase comes from Stephen Mulhall's excellent commentary, *Heidegger and Being and Time (Routledge Philosophy Guidebooks)* (London: Routledge, 1996, 2nd ed 2005) chapter 5 'Theology Secularized: Morality, Guilt and Conscience'.
34. See, for example, the 1924 lectures 'The Problem of Sin in Luther' in *Supplements* 105–110.
35. QCT 35/VA 40.
36. What precisely it means to live in a secular age has recently been explored in great detail by Charles Taylor in *A Secular Age* (Cambridge, MA: Belknap Harvard, 2007). Taylor frequently draws upon Heidegger's thought in his attempt to tackle this problem. He argues, for example, that secularity is essentially bound up with a particular conception of time as homogenous and empty that does not fit easily with Heidegger's understanding of temporality, although he suggests that in the end, 'Heideggerian temporality is also a mode of secular time.' 798, fn 45.
37. PRL 79/112.
38. 'Phenomenology and Theology' in PM 51/63.
39. The term comes from Kant, who uses it to designate a particular kind of theology that believes it can know the existence of God through concepts alone CPR A632/ B660. Heidegger's use of the term is quite different, designating as it does a structure he finds repeated in metaphysical thinking as a whole. See, Iain D. Thompson, *Heidegger on Ontotheology: Technology and the Politics of Education* (Cambridge: University of Cambridge Press, 2005) esp. chapter 1.
40. PM 340/449.
41. One of the most important texts in which Heidegger tries to work out the implications of the 'abysal ground' and the possibility of experiencing the divine that accompanies it is *Contributions to Philosophy (from Enowning)*, See, CP esp. part V 'Grounding' and part VI 'The Last God'.

## CHAPTER 9: ORIGIN AND ORIGINALITY

1. BT 30/10, 375/427.
2. BT 445/393.

3. BT 44/22.
4. BT 44/22.
5. PIA 25/32.
6. René Descartes, *Meditations on First Philosophy*, ed. John Cottingham (Cambridge: Cambridge University Press, 1996) 12.
7. BT 46/25. The destructive research that supports this conclusion is to be found in part two of the 1922–24 lectures *Introduction to Phenomenological Research*. IPR 79–186.
8. HCT 7/9–10.
9. BPP §5.
10. BPP 23/32.
11. FCM 260/378.
12. BT 437/386.
13. BT 437–438/386.
14. PRL 77/109.
15. BT 437–438/385–386.
16. Leopold von Ranke, *History of the Latin and Teutonic Peoples from 1494 to 1514*, Preface to the first edition, in G. G. Iggers and K. von Moltke (eds.), *The Theory and Practice of History* (Indianapolis: Bobbs-Merrill, 1973) 137.
17. BT 437/385.
18. BT 436/384.
19. BT 435/383–384.
20. BT 436–437/384–385.
21. SAGU 2–11.
22. BT 436/384.
23. OBT 66/81.
24. OBT 68/83.
25. OBT 69/84.
26. CP 120/171.
27. CP 121/172.
28. CP 120/171.
29. CP 131/188.
30. BQP 156/180–1.

## CHAPTER 10: ART AND SCIENCE: POETRY AND THOUGHT

1. C. P. Snow, *The Two Cultures*, new edition with introduction by Stefan Collini (Cambridge: Cambridge University Press, 1998).
2. OTL 124/255, PLT 210.
3. For an excellent account of both these and other developments that influenced Heidegger's approach to historical meaning, see Jeffery

Andrew Barash, *Martin Heidegger and the Problem of Historical Meaning* (New York: Fordham University Press, 2003) esp. Chapter 1.
4. Max Weber, *The Methodology of the Social Sciences*, trans. E. A. Shils and H. A. Finch. (New York: Free Press, 1949), 90.
5. See, Wilhelm Dilthey, 'The Formation of the Historical World in the Human Sciences' In R. A. Makkreel and F. Rodi (eds), *Selected Works* Vol. 3, (Princeton: Princeton University Press, 2002).
6. Supplements 60.
7. Supplements 174.
8. Supplements 175–6.
9. PS 19/28.
10. PS 15–16/ 21–22.
11. PS 22–24/ 31–35.
12. PS 26/36–38.
13. PS 26/37.
14. BCP 107/151.
15. BCP 108/152–153.
16. BCP 113/160.
17. BCP 115–116/163–164.
18. CP 92/131.
19. CP 99/143.
20. CP 93/133–134.
21. Theodor W. Adorno and Max Horkheimer, *Dialectic of Enlightenment* (London: Verso, 1997), 120–168. Despite Adorno's frequent criticism of Heidegger, e.g., in *The Jargon of Authenticity* (London: Routledge, 2003), there are many points of comparison between these two thinkers.
22. CP 108/155.
23. QCT 19/VA 23.
24. QCT 17/VA 20.
25. OCT 33/VA38.
26. QCT 156/VA 41.
27. QCT 180/VA 65.
28. QCT 180/VA 65.
29. Aristotle, *Nichomachean Ethics* VI, 2 1140a1–23.
30. OBT 46/61.
31. OWL 101/ 208.

# FURTHER READING

## READERS

Martin Heidegger, *Basic Writings*, ed. David Farrell Krell, revised and expanded edition (London: Routledge, 1993)
Martin Heidegger, *The Heidegger Reader*, ed. Günter Figal (Bloomington: Indiana University Press, 2009)

## HEIDEGGER'S LIFE AND WORK

Rüdiger Safranski, *Martin Heidegger: Between Good and Evil*, trans. Ewald Osers (Cambridge, MA: Harvard University Press, 1998)

## INTRODUCTIONS

Willliam Blattner, *Heidegger's 'Being and Time'* (London: Continuum, 2006)
Miguel de Beistegui, *The New Heidegger* (London: Continuum, 2005)
Stephen Mulhall, *Heidegger and 'Being and Time'*, 2nd edn (London: Routledge, 2005)
Julian Young, *Heidegger's Later Philosophy* (Cambridge: Cambridge University Press, 2002)

## CRITICAL COLLECTIONS

Hubert L. Dreyfus and Mark A. Wrathall (eds), *A Companion to Heidegger*, 2nd edn (Oxford: Blackwell, 2007)
Charles B. Guignon (ed.), *The Cambridge Companion to Heidegger*, 2nd edn (Cambridge: Cambridge University Press, 2006)

## PHENOMENOLOGY AND BEYOND

Steven Galt Crowell, *Husserl, Heidegger and the Space of Meaning* (Evaston: Northwestern University Press, 2001)

William McNeill, *The Glance of the Eye: Heidegger, Aristotle, and the Ends of Theory* (Albany, NY: State University of New York Press, 1999)

## ENVIRONMENT, NATURE AND EMBODIMENT

Bruce V. Foltz, *Inhabiting the Earth: Heidegger, Environmental Ethics, and the Metaphysics of Nature* (New Jersey: Humanities Press, 2005)
Ladelle McWhorter and Gail Stenstad (eds), *Heidegger and the Earth: Essays in Environmental Philosophy*, second expanded edition (Toronto: University of Toronto Press, 2009)
Frank Schalow, *The Incarnality of Being: The Earth, Animals, and the Body in Heidegger's Thought* (Albany, NY: State University of New York Press, 2006)

## ETHICS AND POLITICS

Miguel de Beistegui, *Heidegger and the Political* (London: Routledge, 1998)
François Raffoul and David Pettigrew (eds), *Heidegger and Practical Philosophy* (Albany, NY: State University of New York Press, 2002)
Richard Wolin (ed.), *The Heidegger Controversy: A Critical Reader* (Cambrdige, MA: MIT Press, 1993)

## TRUTH

Daniel O. Dahlstrom, *Heidegger's Concept of Truth* (Cambridge: Cambridge University Press, 1994)

## SPACE AND TIME

Françoise Dastur, *Heidegger and the Question of Time*, trans. François Raffoul and David Pettigrew (Atlantic Highlands: Humanities Press, 1998)
Jeff Malpus, *Heidegger's Topology. Being Place, World* (Cambridge, MA: MIT Press, 2006)

## RELIGION AND THE SACRED

Benjamin D. Crowe, *Heidegger's Religious Origins: Destruction and Authenticity* (Bloomington: Indiana University Press, 2005)
Laurence Paul Hemming, *Heidegger's Atheism. The Refusal of a Theological Voice* (Notre Dame, Indiana: University of Notre Dame Press, 2002)

## HISTORICITY, CULTURE AND TECHNOLOGY

Jeffrey Andrew Barash, *The Problem of Historical Meaning*, revised and expanded edition (New York: Fordham University Press, 2003)

Iain D. Thomson, *Heidegger on Ontotheology: Technology and the Politics of Education* (Cambridge: Cambridge University Press, 2005)

# BIBLIOGRAPHY

*For works by Heidegger cited in the text see the Abbreviations section above.*

Adorno, Theodor W. *The Jargon of Authenticity* (London: Routledge, 2003).

Adorno, Theodor W. and Max Horkheimer. *Dialectic of Enlightenment* (London: Verso, 1997).

Allison, Henry E. *Kant's Transcendental Idealism: An Interpretation and Defence*, 2nd edn (New Haven: Yale University Press, 2004).

Aristotle, *The Complete Works of Aristotle*, ed. Jonathan Barnes (Princeton: Princeton University Press).

Barash, Jeffery Andrew. *Martin Heidegger and the Problem of Historical Meaning*, revised and expanded edition (New York: Fordham University Press, 2003).

Beckett, Samuel. *Three Occasional Pieces* (London: Faber and Faber, 1982).

de Beistegui. *Heidegger and the Political* (London: Routledge, 1998).

—. *The New Heidegger* (London: Continuum, 2005).

Bergson, Henri. *Creative Evolution*, trans. Arthur Mitchell (Mineola, New York: Dover, 1998).

Blattner, William. *Heidegger's 'Being and Time'* (London: Continuum, 2006).

Collingwood, R. G. *An Autobiography* (Oxford: Oxford University Press, 1978).

Crowe, Benjamin D. *Heidegger's Religious Origins: Destruction and Authenticity* (Bloomington: Indiana University Press, 2005).

Crowell, Steven Galt. *Husserl, Heidegger and the Space of Meaning* (Evaston Ill.: Northwestern University Press, 2001).

Dahlstrom, Daniel O. *Heidegger's Concept of Truth* (Cambridge: Cambridge University Press, 1994).

Dastur, Françoise. *Heidegger and the Question of Time*, trans. François Raffoul and David Pettigrew (Atlantic Highlands: Humanities Press, 1998).

Derrida, Jacques. 'Geschlecht: sexual difference, ontological difference' *Research in Phenomenology* (Vol. 13, No.1, 1983) 65–83.

Descartes, René. *Meditations on First Philosophy*, ed. John Cottingham (Cambridge: Cambridge University Press, 1996).

Dilthey, Wilhelm. 'The Formation of the Historical World in the Human Sciences' In R. A. Makkreel and F. Rodi (eds), *Selected Works* Vol.3, (Princeton: Princeton University Press, 2002).

Dreyfus, Hubert L. and Mark A. Wrathall (eds). *A Companion to Heidegger*, 2nd edn (Oxford: Blackwell, 2007).

Foltz, Bruce V. *Inhabiting the Earth: Heidegger, Environmental Ethics, and the Metaphysics of Nature* (New Jersey: Humanities Press, 2005).

Guignon, Charles B. (ed.). *The Cambridge Companion to Heidegger*, 2nd edn (Cambridge: Cambridge University Press, 2006).

Haar, Michel. *The Song of the Earth: Heidegger and the Grounds of the History of Being*, trans. Reginald Lilly (Bloomington: Indiana University Press, 1993).

Hemming, Laurence Paul. *Heidegger's Atheism. The Refusal of a Theological Voice* (Notre Dame, Indiana: University of Notre Dame Press, 2002).

Husserl, Edmund. *Ideas Pertaining to a Pure Phenomenology and to Phenomenological Philosophy, First Book*, trans. Fred Kersten (Dordrecht: Kluwer, 1998).

—. *Logical Investigations*, Vol II, trans. J. N. Findlay (London: Routledge, 2001).

—. 'Philosophy as a Rigorous Science' in Peter McCormick and Frederick A. Elliston (eds), *Husserl: Shorter Works*, (Notre Dame, Indiana: University of Notre Dame Press, 1981).

—. *The Phenomenology of Internal Time-Consciousness*, trans. James C. Churchill (Bloomington: Indiana University Press, 1964).

Iggers, G. G. and K. von Moltke (eds). *The Theory and Practice of History* (Indianapolis: Bobbs-Merrill, 1973).

Kierkegaard, Søren. *The Concept of Anxiety*, trans. Reidar Thomte and Albert B. Anderson (Princeton: Princeton University Press, 1980).

—. *Sickness unto Death*, trans. Howard V. Hong and Edna H. Hong (Princeton: Princeton University Press, 1980).

Kiesel, Theodore. *The Genesis of Being and Time* (Berkeley: University of California Press, 1993).

Malpus, Jeff. *Heidegger's Topology. Being, Place, World* (Cambridge, MA: MIT Press, 2006).

McNeill, William. *The Glance of the Eye: Heidegger, Aristotle, and the Ends of Theory* (Albany, NY: State University of New York Press, 1999).

McWhorter, Ladelle. and Gail Stenstad (eds). *Heidegger and the Earth: Essays in Environmental Philosophy*, second expanded edition (Toronto: University of Toronto Press, 2009).

Merleau-Ponty, Maurice. *Nature: Course Notes from the Collège de France*, trans. Robert Vallier (Evaston Ill.: Northwestern University Press, 2003).

Mulhall, Stephen. *Heidegger and Being and Time* (*Routledge Philosophy Guidebooks*) (London: Routledge, 1996, 2nd edn 2005).

Nietzsche, Friedrich. *The Gay Science,* trans. Walter Kaufmann (New York: Vintage, 1974).

—. *On the Genealogy of Morals and Ecce Homo*, trans. Walter Kaufmann (New York: Vintage, 1969).

## BIBLIOGRAPHY

Novalis. *Novalis: Philosophical Writings*, trans. Margaret Mahony Stoljar (Albany, N.Y.: State University of New York Press, 1997).

Raffoul, François and David Pettigrew (eds). *Heidegger and Practical Philosophy* (Albany, NY: State University of New York Press, 2002).

Safranski, Rüdiger. *Martin Heidegger: Between Good and Evil*, trans. Ewald Osers (Cambridge, MA: Harvard University Press, 1998).

Schalow, Frank. *The Incarnality of Being: The Earth, Animals, and the Body in Heidegger's Thought* (Albany, NY: State University of New York Press, 2006).

Snow, C. P. *The Two Cultures*, new edition with introduction by Stefan Collini (Cambridge: Cambridge University Press, 1998).

Svendsen, Lars. *The Philosophy of Boredom*, trans. John Irons (London: Reacktion Books, 2005).

Taylor, Charles. *A Secular Age* (Cambridge, MA: Belknap Harvard, 2007).

Thompson, Iain D. *Heidegger on Ontotheology: Technology and the Politics of Education* (Cambridge: University of Cambridge Press, 2005).

Weber, Max. *The Methodology of the Social Sciences*, trans. E. A. Shils and H. A. Finch (New York: Free Press, 1949).

Wittgenstein, Ludwig. *Tractatus Logico-Philosophicus*, trans. C. K. Ogden (London: Routledge, 1996).

Wolin, Richard (ed.). *The Heidegger Controversy: A Critical Reader* (Cambridge, MA: MIT Press, 1993).

Young, Julian. *Heidegger's Later Philosophy* (Cambridge: Cambridge University Press, 2002).

# INDEX

bold entries refer to the most important discussion